SONGS AND STORIES FROM A CANADIAN YOOPER

Mike McCarthy

SCRIPTOR HOUSE
THE EPITOME OF GREATNESS

Scriptor House LLC

2810 N Church St Wilmington, Delaware, 19802

www.scriptorhouse.com

Phone: +1302-205-2043

Published by Scriptor House LLC

Paperback ISBN: 979-8-88692-301-8

eBook ISBN: 979-8-88692-302-5

Hardback ISBN: 979-8-88692-307-0

Table of Contents

Statement

All proceeds from the sale of my book ***"Songs and Stories from a Canadian Yooper"*** will be donated to the Bruce Township Historical Library for their continued purpose and expansion. This entity was organized to bring forth the history of Bruce Township and surrounding towns and villages, as well as the historical significance to the people of their region.

Foreword

For the past twenty-five years, my passion has been to collect as much of the history of Bruce Township, here in the Upper Peninsula of Michigan. I really felt a deep concern for not only the kids of today, but future generations, so they will know about our local history, and " how life was back then." I didn't realize how much was missing, and I found, we had our work cut out for us. So, I began to speak out publicly with every chance I could, of the importance of preserving our past, as well as our local history.

Mike McCarthy heard of my local historical interest through a mutual friend, so he called and asked me to assist him in his book, *Songs and Stories from a Canadian Yooper*. I thought that this would be perfect. Before I even met Mike, I read his two earlier books about his childhood in, *The Sounds and Smells of My Childhood*, and truly enjoyed his memoirs. I felt he was very authentic and wrote with great humor. He touched some sad notes with some tears but proved to me that he was an excellent storyteller . Then when we met, it was like wearing a comfortable old shoe— we clicked! How great it was to meet and find someone with an equal passion as myself and record our history with stories together. So, I jumped in and offered my help, and I must say how much fun it was.

The reader will enjoy his sharing of his trip around the Upper Peninsula of Michigan, and the subsequent stories that follow. The many storytellers and folks he met along the way are worth remembering. By the time you've finished the book, you will know what a Canadian Yooper is, and that was his goal. In many ways, his book is a family story, as well as his own. He refers throughout to his great-grandparents who were early settlers in the Upper Peninsula and his grandparents that helped to raise him, and the love of his mom and dad.

You'll find it to be an amazing road he's traveled, filled with stories and tales, all kinds of local history. While the aged pictures he inserts in his book really help the reader to fully understand how things were. It all tells a story.

As a local historian, here in Bruce Township, I really like it. As much as I get discouraged when I see or hear of people throwing old pictures in their trash or throwing away older newspapers . I must admit I get really encouraged when folks like Mike take the time to research, do their homework, and then write about our history. *Songs and Stories from a Canadian Yooper* is an exceptional piece of work, of our local history. I'm sure as you read it, it will cause more than a laugh or two. So, enjoy your reading, and then join us, or join your own local group of historians to preserve our precious past. Let's give our history to future generations.

Mrs. Shirley Patrick, Bruce Township Historian Bruce Township

Prelude

This is the third book in a trilogy, enjoying, while examining the adventures and memoirs of several generations of one American family, the McCarthy's. It is seen through the eyes of its author, Mike McCarthy. It's set amidst the times of nostalgia of the 1950s, then through the author's own personal journey of his alcoholic addiction, and finally, his Songs and Stories, he weaves looking back on his life, and some of the amazing recollections of it. *'The Sounds and Smells of My Childhood'*, *'My Road to Sobriety'*, and *'Songs and Stories from a Canadian Yooper"*, each are cut from the same thread with a similar purpose that integrity and gratitude matter. I hope you enjoy reading them.

Introduction

Before I begin my story, I owe it to those who, like me, claim to be Canadian Yoopers. It is simply defined really. It is an individual who is born and raised in the Upper Peninsula of Michigan, with Canadian ancestry,— in most cases, French- Canadian. I'll explain further in the book, but our portion of the UP namely our three Eastern Counties were once a part of Upper Canada. Some of us were Irish, Scottish, or Italian, while some of us were Greek, or Polish, and some were German. A small number of us were Lebanese and Jewish. We too had our Finnish and Swedes, and we had several Dutch settlers. The locals would say, "We were 'bred and buttered' in the Soo Region of the EUP," and if you weren't of native origin, you were an Immigrant to our Land called the Upper Peninsula. So, yes, we too are Yoopers. Different in our ancestry than most of the Yoopers in the Western UP, but we sound more Canadian, and although our dialect is similar but separate, the characteristics of all Canadian Yoopers are similar as well, but with a little more Canadian civility to us.

In the summer of 2005, for the very first time, I took a 2 week road trip around the UP. I visited the Ten largest communities in the Upper Peninsula of Michigan while driving the Lake Superior coastline from the Sault to the UP's largest city in Marquette, with a stopover in Munising and Seney. I really wanted those few hours in Seney, as that was really like an old West town. It was called as "tough, two- fisted a town as any on earth." The town became a hotbed for fights, booze, prostitution, killings, and gambling. It was named after a NY Banker, and railroad builder, George Seney. Can you imagine over 3,000 lumberjacks and 15 lumber companies operating there in Seney's sandy soil cutting the huge White Pine? To service these people, Seney offered ten hotels, a dozen saloons, several blind pigs (unlicensed bars), a Catholic Church, a school, two large general merchandise stores, several drug stores, meat markets and jewelry stores. My Grandfather, Pop, was one of the 3,000 lumberjacks earning $1.25 per day. But his stories and his memories and remembrances working there were golden and worth remembering.

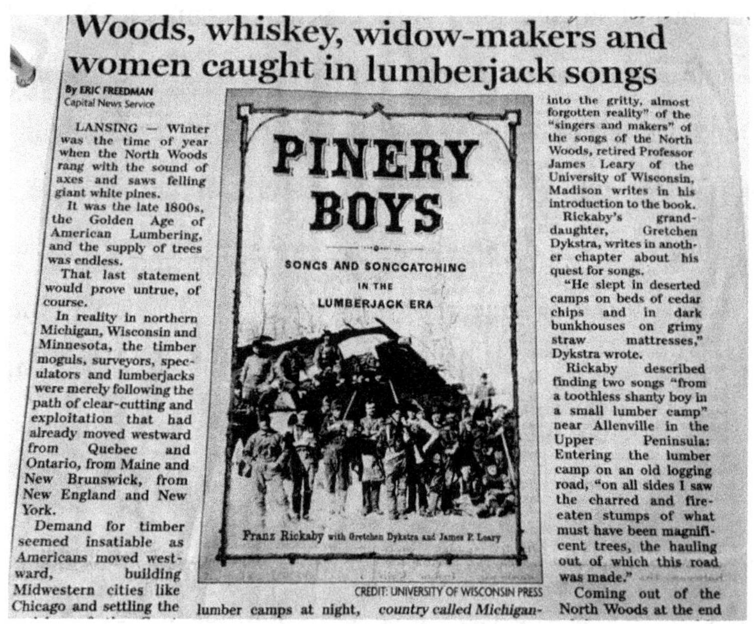

Woods, whiskey, widow-makers and women caught in lumberjack songs

By ERIC FREEDMAN
Capital News Service

LANSING — Winter was the time of year when the North Woods rang with the sound of axes and saws felling giant white pines.

It was the late 1800s, the Golden Age of American Lumbering, and the supply of trees was endless.

That last statement would prove untrue, of course.

In reality in northern Michigan, Wisconsin and Minnesota, the timber moguls, surveyors, speculators and lumberjacks were merely following the path of clear-cutting and exploitation that had already moved westward from Quebec and Ontario, from Maine and New Brunswick, from New England and New York.

Demand for timber seemed insatiable as Americans moved westward, building Midwestern cities like Chicago and settling the

into the gritty, almost forgotten reality" of the "singers and makers" of the songs of the North Woods, retired Professor James Leary of the University of Wisconsin, Madison writes in his introduction to the book.

Rickaby's granddaughter, Gretchen Dykstra, writes in another chapter about his quest for songs.

"He slept in deserted camps on beds of cedar chips and in dark bunkhouses on grimy straw mattresses," Dykstra wrote.

Rickaby described finding two songs "from a toothless shanty boy in a small lumber camp" near Allenville in the Upper Peninsula: Entering the lumber camp on an old logging road, "on all sides I saw the charred and fire-eaten stumps of what must have been magnificent trees, the hauling out of which this road was made."

Coming out of the North Woods at the end

lumber camps at night, *country called Michigan-*

Bruce Township Library Collection

I did have a great visit with family and a lengthy historic chat of the City's Cleveland Cliffs Ore Dock. I did a lot of research there in Marquette. I remember well the great Marquette Iron Rangers playing our original Soo Indians in hockey in the 1950s . I then drove directly to Copper Harbor in the Keweenaw Peninsula . I stopped and chatted and hung out there . I learned very quickly in a local diner, in its heyday in the latter half of the 19th century and the early 20th century, the area was the world's greatest producer of copper. The next day, driving south through the Houghton-Hancock region onward to Ironwood. I spent a few days over there as well collecting whatever I could from the historical societies and just networking at diners, and small cafes with the locals. Of special interest to me were the great Calumet Fire in the early 1900s, and The Miners Strike . The fire is famous in a song by Woody Guthrie . It is to this day called, The Italian Hall Disaster (sometimes referred to as the 1913 Massacre)— a tragedy that occurred on Wednesday, December 24, 1913, in Calumet, where seventy -three people, mostly striking mine workers and their families, were crushed to death in a stampede when someone falsely yelled fire at a crowded Christmas Party. A dear friend of my father's lived in Calumet during that period, and his father was a striker, when the company bosses of the Calumet Hecla mine with their paid thugs and police beat up hundreds of the striking workers and their families. Bill Murphy was just 9 years old. He was standing in a picket line with his father and was hit with a club, beaten over his head several times, and needed 17 stitches and a three-day hospital stay. It left a mighty scar on his forehead, and a lesson he would never forget. He later moved to the Sault, married, and raised two children. He became a labor leader at our local Tannery in the Sault, a major employer, with their Fur and Leather Workers Union. Bill became the National Treasurer of the National Union. He loved telling his stories of traveling by train out east to New Jersey. He was great fun to listen to . I then drove south again to Iron Mountain and Menominee, which is an amazing historic and busy industrial market. I enjoyed my time there and learned of the several bridges spanning across the Montreal River that attach Wisconsin to the UP.

Finally, I followed the Lake Michigan coastline through Escanaba, which I found interesting, and Gladstone and Manistique to the Mackinac Bridge. It was along this road I heard old stories of logging white pine, and tales of how life was during the Prohibition, and where the stills were located. It was great fun. The final two days I followed the Lake Huron coastline through Hessel then Cedarville, and DeTour when the broad majestic St. Mary's River took me back through Stalwart, Raber, and Barbeau to the Sault. What an amazing trip. I learned so much, saw things I've never seen, and heard some of the greatest stories I was ever told about my home, the UP. I believe, to this day, some of the greatest storytellers in the world come from here. Back then, I was doing my research and doing the prep work for hopefully a book I could write. I stopped just after I had started to write. It has finally come full circle, I'm writing it today. The name of the book is called, 'Songs and Stories from a Canadian Yooper'. I began to focus on the three Counties of the Eastern Upper Peninsula. Looking at our historic ties to Canada and dating back years to the French Jesuit explorers proved to me that we really were once a part of French Canada. The Jay Treaty of 1794 and the Boundary Commission following the War of 1812 changed everything.

The old French Fur Trading ways of doing things with great relations with the local Native tribes were coming to an end. It was the Boundary Commission for England and the United States and the quarrel with Ohio over Toledo that led to the creation of the Upper Peninsula as Michigan became a state in the 1820s, and no longer just a territory. But I also wanted first to define for myself this new identity of the term Yooper. Who we are and what traits we seem to share as a unit of the State of Michigan. I also visited two Native American Reservations. The first was in L'Anse, The Keweenaw Bay Indian Community of Lake Superior Chippewa Indians. The second, The Bay Mills Indian Community of Anishinaabe Indians, in Bay Mills, Michigan. I then believed I could weave a story.

The Upper Peninsula, as we who live there and are native to it know full well of its beauty, its people and its promise. It's amazing when you think of it having 1,700 coastal miles from the three lakes: Superior, Michigan, and Huron. From DeTour on the far East to the UP's far West of Ironwood, it's over 350 miles, and then driving back to St. Ignace on the south Michigan shore, is another 320 miles. So, it's an easy ride, filled with pleasure and lots of fun. The drive of 720 miles took me just 12 days.

The UP has 15 Counties and a population of 320,000 or just 3% of the state of Michigan's total. It has 10 major cities and towns with approximately 205,500 people that live in towns with 2,000 people or fewer . The ten large towns and cities are:

- Marquette (19,661)

- Sault Ste. Marie (16,542)

- Escanaba (13,140)

- Menominee (9,131)

- Iron Mountain (8,154)

- Houghton (7,134)

- Ishpeming (6,535)

- Ironwood (6,293)

- Kingsford (5,549)

- Gladstone (5,266)

The UP Town & Village Map, Wikipedia

The Yooper term itself, I found to be interesting. On August 5th, 1979, the Escanaba Daily Press hosted a competition for people to join and come up with the best word to describe residents of Michigan's Upper Peninsula. For those out there who have laughed at the word Yooper, look at some of the other nominations that day in the newspaper.

Skeeter-eater (as in mosquitoes)

Michupper

Bush turkey

Pastian (as in pasty)

After seeing a few of the other submissions, Yooper seemed to be as good of choice as any. Brett Crawford of Bark River was credited with submitting the term Yooper, and he will forever go down in history as a legend, creating one of the greatest influences in Upper Peninsula history. Clearly, Yooper is derived from the abbreviation of Upper Peninsula (U.P.) plus "-er". As in, "He's a U.P.-er". Bailey reported that the Pittsburgh Press used the term spelled U.P.-er in a 1987 edition. That was 37 years ago.

Today, the term Yooper is still being published in mass media.

As I was doing my research on the word Yooper, I also found it wasn't until 2014 that Yoopers were officially recognized by the rest of the United States. A gentleman by the name of Steve Parks, a Delta County resident, had a major play in its being placed properly in the Webster Dictionary. It was he who decided if he could get it in the dictionary.

For more than 10 years, Steve Parks wrote to Merriam-Webster under the pen name Clayton Parks. He says he tried to have some fun with his work by sending the lexicographer some Yooper treats. He tried everything he could think of, but it was a crossword puzzle that made all the difference.

"A crossword puzzle from the Boston Globe and the word was 'a name for a resident of the Upper Peninsula of Michigan' and that was probably the clincher," he adds.

So, there you have it, I'm a Yooper, but to be more clear, I'm a Canadian Yooper . There are thousands of us here, mostly in the EUP, some scattered throughout the UP and Michigan, and the rest throughout our Country. It's a little funny, as a kid and younger adult, that I always referred to myself as being from the UP of Michigan to differentiate myself from the rest of the State in the Lower Peninsula. In fact, prior to the brilliant construction of the Mackinac Bridge which opened in 1957, we were a divided state, with a number of folks living in the UP wanting state independence and the creation of the State of Superior. But with the construction and opening of the Mackinac Bridge, the economic ties to Detroit and to the many cities and towns of Lower Michigan began to open up and the socio-economic ties began. In the western UP, ties with Wisconsin were also strengthened. The bridge lessened some of the economic influence from Canada as the ferry boat system and family ties kept that relationship strong overall but still weakened. Not until 1962 did things begin to show improved results. We had another brilliant piece of construction with the opening of the International Bridge across our St. Mary's river, which tied the two Saults of Michigan and Ontario together. Today, over 1.9 million vehicles a year pass over that bridge, and have had a great impact on the cultural and economic society of Sault Michigan. Again, hence, Canadian Yoopers are here to stay.

A great deal has been discussed regarding our UP dialect, and yes, it is heavily influenced by Scandinavian folklore. But the French-Canadian influence too is very distinctive, and always has been, even before one Scandinavian placed one foot in the Upper Peninsula. What you'll hear in the Upper Peninsula of Michigan is a different dialect. The accent is heavily influenced by the area's immigrants from Finland, Sweden, Italy, Ireland, Cornwall, and French Canada. So, here we will say, 'yah' instead of yeah, "d" for "th" and 'eh' at the end of most sentences. As kids, we would end our alphabet with the letter zed, not zee. It was different in school as we would hear both uses of English, Canadian, and American. Words such as Process not Pracess, Project not Praject, Agane (again), not Agan. A few of us made the mistake in school of saying the word schedule not Skedhule. There were all very little things but obvious with the differences. The best part was that the characteristics of a Yooper remained almost the same. Yoopers are very kind and resilient, they are hardy, not afraid of work, harmonious, and are connected to their homeland. We are a tight-knit bunch and know how to survive and keep a smile in a two-foot snowstorm. We love fishing, but hunting is our ultimate joy. They love a cold beer.

I, like thousands of others with me, am very proud to call ourselves Canadian Yoopers. In my case, it was easy. My father's family on both sides came from Ireland through Canada, while my mother's were all born in Sault in Ontario, Canada. It was easy and appropriate for me to hold citizenship in both countries, which I do today. Here are some of my songs and stories

. I hope you enjoy them. I have extended an invitation to members of my family, namely John McDonald, my cousin, and dear friends, Tony Andary and Barbara Hallesy Wirt, to participate as co-authors in my book and contribute a chapter. The boys and their stories of fishing and hunting back home are humorous and exciting. Each year, Tony tags a deer at their deer camp in Chippewa County. John and his son Ethan are avid fishermen and know the Saint Mary's River and how to fish it as well as anyone. The walleye and salmon that John and his son Ethan catch will amaze you, and Tony going to a deer camp called Jo Bo-Do every year is just simply entertaining to hear. Barbara, I've asked her to give us a history of how Hallesy's Bar came to life. This was one of the very best saloons ever. You may have seen the TV series CHEERS, well many years before it was even a thought, there was Hallesy's Bar. I know you'll enjoy reading their chapters.

Finally, a great story I was told by my dear friend Paul Byron before he passed away, may he rest in peace, is really worth reading. He uncovered a 61-year-old error in the Michigan Sports Records showing that in 1963 Loretto Catholic from the Sault tied with St. Ignace in a football game by a score of 13-13. So instead of an undefeated season, which we were one of 4 UP teams that year to accomplish, the state of Michigan disavowed any wrongdoing, and their UP office recorded the game correctly. They have refused to change their records. Paul went on to prove by collecting news records and clippings, as well as personal interviews, that Loretto won the football game 33-13. As I said, it is recorded wrongly in our State Records. But they wouldn't accept his request to change what he called a "grammatical error" or accept his material. They certainly didn't know Paul Byron. Since he was a kid once his jaw was set. He was not going to back down. He began setting up his appeal to the State just as we were meeting for the 50th annual Loretto reunion of our class of 1966. He told me everything, and after our chat, I encouraged him to get after it. Not only that, but he was doing that very thing when his illness occurred, and he died. So, we, his friends, have taken up his fight. But his story is a gem. I know you will enjoy it.

CHAPTER 1

The Car Ferries

Webster's Dictionary states that a Peninsula is a piece of land surrounded on three sides by water. That's certainly the way it is in the Eastern Upper Peninsula. On the North side is the largest freshwater lake in the world, now referred to as an Inland Sea, but to us, it's our Lake Superior. It then meets with the Rapids of St. Mary in the Sault, extends itself to Lake Huron, and then flows to the Straits of Mackinac, where it then meets with Lake Michigan. It is safe to say that we are a land of Water, Bridges, and Ferry Boats. In the EUP, we had ferry systems operating across the St. Mary's river connecting both Saults, then we had ferries to the islands of Sugar Island, Neebish Island, Mackinac Island, and Drummond Island. But the big one was the granddaddy of them all, the one connecting the Upper and Lower Peninsulas of Michigan. The ferry that left St. Ignace and landed in Mackinaw City, is operated by the Michigan State Highway Department.

Each one is worth chatting about, but for me, I spent a lot of my time growing up in the 1950s visiting my mother's family in Sault Ontario and taking the ferry connecting our two Saults. Sometimes it was the ferry boat named Curran or the other, The McPhail. The adventure begins with a one mile ferry ride across the very beautiful, broad, majestic St. Mary's river. The ferry could hold up to 24 cars if they were small. It crossed the river every hour, bringing cars, passengers, trucks, and semi-trucks across to the docks in both Saults. There were no advance ticket sales. Many times, and I mean many times, the waiting lines for parked cars along Water Street and Portage Street on our Michigan side could be very lengthy, measured in hours just sitting in your car in the queue. It wasn't that way all the time, but on weekends or special holidays, you better get there early or stay busy waiting.

The ferry system to both Saults had an interesting history. It began in the 1870s, many years ago now, when the first ferry, Grace, transported passengers (four per trip) across the St. Mary's River between the "two Soo's." A Sault Michigan man, the late Captain Charles Ripley, who was connected with every ferry on the St. Mary's, except the last two, built the Grace in 1873. The boat had a steam engine and was 24 feet long and comparable in size to the standard lifeboats carried on the Great Lakes freighters of today. The crew consisted of Captain Ripley, George Masters, the chief engineer, and his wife, who assisted as the pilot. They operated The Grace for several years. Many boats followed after that, varying in size when Captain Ripley purchased The Flora Holden which he operated for ten years before it was shut down.

Several smaller boats filled the gap when Ripley acquired an 80-foot steam ferry, The International, built in Buffalo, NY in 1889.

FLORA HOLDEN

By the time he and his team sailed the boat back to the Sault, he was met with some competition, as J.J. Bevkeith was placed on the river. The first competition Ripley encountered. But, after a year, the two operators joined forces, using both boats. Finally, The Beckwith was sold, converted to a tug, and was later wrecked on Lake Superior.

Two smaller ships, Ivanhoe and Mascot, joined with The International to make a fleet of three ferries in service between the two Soo's. Three ferries which were not used again for over fifty years until John A. McPhail was added to the James W. Curran and Algoming in 1955. The Ivanhoe ended her career as a ferry by burning at the dock, and The June Hagarty was purchased to be used with the mascot . At about the same time, The Soo Ferryboat Company was formed. Captain Ripley retired as an active ferryboat.

INTERNATIONAL

The International was sold to a group operating in Lake Superior and met her fate by fire at the dock in Houghton, Michigan.

The Thomas Friant was next in line and was used both as a ferry and an excursion boat but was sold when the International Transit Company was formed in 1901. Before the formation of the new company, The Mascot and Hagarty, were sold, The Fortune was purchased, and Captain Ripley became dock manager of the new firm. This new company purchased The Algoma, a side-loading steamer built in 1899 in Toronto, Ontario, and used it along with The Fortune until 1910, when the latter was sold. The Algoma carried on the ferry service between the two Soo's until 1926. She was 124 feet long with a beam of 26 feet, and after her busy career as a ferry, she became a package freighter on the St. Lawrence River, at one time during this period the fare for foot passengers crossing The St. Mary's was ten cents each way, and for horned cattle, twenty-five cents.

The first diesel car ferry, The Agoming was built in Collingwood, Ontario, and went into service in 1926, ending operations with the opening of the new International Bridge in 1962.

More automobiles, improved highways, and an ever-growing tourist trade, along with the increasing population of the two Soo's, soon made additional ferry service a necessity, thus The James W. Curran and The John A. McPhail were added in 1947 and 1955, respectively, both terminating service with the opening of the bridge. It was The McPhail and The Curran that I remember well, as all passengers could leave their parked cars and stand on the top deck and enjoy the ride across the river.

J.W. CURRAN

AGOMING

The Ontario Government purchased the ferry service for $1,650,000.00 in June 1960. While the Province of Ontario was operating the ferries from June 1960 to October 1962, the greatest number of cars ever carried crossed on August 18, 1962, when 3,425 cars were transported across the St. Mary's River. At first, The Agoming could carry up to 24 cars, but as they increased in size, she finally was limited to 12 to 16 cars per trip.

Before the 24-hour ferry service was established, anyone wishing to cross the St. Mary's River in winter after regular ferry hours had to walk the ice, following a row of evergreen trees stuck in the snow to mark a path. The water on the Canadian side being faster did not freeze as quickly as the remainder of the river, so a small boat was used to ferry people across the open stretch of water. This proved to be profitable business, especially on Sunday, the busiest day of the week. At first, the ferry service operated only during the navigation season with the last trip at 8 p.m. This was changed to 9 p.m., then 11, and finally 1 a.m., before the 24-hour and 12-month service became a reality.

The ferry system has been a vital part of the history and progress of the Two Saults and regions. During the few years before the opening of the bridge, the inadequacy of any type of ferry transportation became increasingly evident. As I mentioned earlier about the line-ups and getting there to the docks early, congested streets became a part of life in both cities; many people had to wait four or five hours to cross the river.

Although the ferries represent the end of an era and the bridge the beginning of a new one, the St. Mary's river, which they both had to overcome, represents all eras—yesterday, today, and tomorrow—as it fulfills its destiny as a link in our great "Inland Seas."

SUGAR ISLAND, NEEBISH, DRUM- MOND, AND MACKINAC ISLANDS.

All the islands have ferry boat services carrying passengers daily back and forth. They all share a unique history.

Sugar Island was part of the Canada—United States border dispute settled by the Webster—Ashburton Treaty and affirmed to be part of the United States when the treaty was signed on August 9, 1842. It had been called St. George's Island by the British, and Maple Sugar Island by the Native Chippewas for its abundant maple trees. Ferry service began in 1925.

Since 1975, the Transportation Authority has provided daily 24-hour service to the island of 600 full-time residents.

The Sugar Islander

Drummond Island with a full-time population today of 1,000 people has a fascinating history. It was the last British outpost on American soil following the Treaty of Ghent (1814). It was finally returned to American hands in 1828. Drummond Island is the only island in the Manitoulin Island chain which is part of the United States. The Ontario island of Manitoulin is the largest freshwater island in the world.

Another unique feature is the ice bridge that forms each year between Drummond Island in Chippewa County and St. Joseph Island in Ontario, Canada during the winter months. Once the ice has frozen to a safe depth, locals can enjoy winter activities on the trails. The bridge opened this year in February. Today, the EUP Transportation Authority provides a daily ferry service to and from the island.

The Drummond Islander

Neebish Island today has 100 full-time residents who live on the island. It is believed to have been named by European settlers from the Ojibwe word aniibiish, meaning "leaf". Following the Anglo-American War of 1812, British and American negotiators agreed to settle long-standing border disputes along the northern border in the Great Lakes area and elsewhere that remained from the treaty following the American Revolutionary War. The ferry service is provided by the Regional Transportation Authority.

Mackinac Island is by far the most interesting of all the islands, not by size or population, but by the number of tourists who visit. It, too, has a fascinating history. First visited by French explorers in the 1600s, the island was an ancient Indian burial ground called Michilimackinac ("Great Turtle") when, because of its strategic location, the British established a fort there in 1780. It was also a major fur trading post founded by Ezekiel Solomon. He was the state's first Jewish citizen and successful fur trader in Michigan. Today, the island is totally a summer resort, with ferry service from both St. Ignace in the Upper Peninsula and Mackinaw City in the Lower Peninsula.

Shepler's Mackinac Island Ferry is one of two ferry companies serving Mackinac Island, Michigan. The company has docks in Mackinaw City and St. Ignace. Shepler's provides ferry and freight service to Mackinac Island. The island, 8 miles (13 km) in circumference and thickly forested, has been a state park since 1895. It retains an 18th- and 19th-century atmosphere; automobiles are banned, and horses, buggies, and bicycles are used for transport. The island was a gathering place for the local tribes, who made offerings to Gitche Manitou. It became the burial place of tribal chiefs.

Mackinac Island is a premiere tourist destination, garnering over one million visitors each year. In 2018, it was named as the number one North American destination by Trip Advisor.

The Shepler family for three generations since 1945, led by founder William Shepler have maintained an operations motto that is specific and meaningful—"Give the best possible service with a smile, use modern equipment and employ a well-trained staff." From the early charter boat days to today, Shepler's approach to transporting people to Mackinac Island has been one of class and value. Throughout the years, Shepler's has undergone several major renovations of the docks and facilities in Mackinaw City, St. Ignace and on Mackinac Island. A successful freight service was added, all the while adhering to the high standards of quality service that have become known throughout the industry worldwide.

THE CAR FERRIES TO THE LOWER PENINSULA.

This was the granddaddy of them all. The ferry system operated by the Michigan Highway Department, and it was special. The car ferry service operated from 1923 until the completion of the Mackinac Bridge in 1957. The state ferry operation was basically a highway over water. It was the first service like this operated by a state highway department. The waiting time wasn't that great, but it really was a great trip. Here are some of those trips and the ships that took us over to the other side.

Vacationland, the newest and largest car ferry, was added to the Straits of Mackinac fleet to improve service between Mackinaw City and St. Ignace, Mich. Date issued: 1930—1945 (approximate)

Before the bridge was built, the only way to cross the straits with vehicles was by using the car ferries. These ferries were owned and operated by the State of Michigan, specifically the Michigan State Highway Department (now the Michigan Department of Transportation). They provided an essential transportation link for motorists traveling between the Upper and Lower Peninsulas. The Michigan State Ferries played a crucial role in providing transportation across the Straits of Mackinac.

Starting in 1923 on through 1957, 9 ships operated across the straits . Over 12 million vehicles and 30 million passengers were serviced between the two communities of St. Ignace and Mackinaw City in that time period.

At one time, the service was seasonal, and then the state bought ice-breaking ships that " crunched through massive ice floes as if they were paper boxes."

What follows are images of the ships and descriptions courtesy of the Mackinac Bridge Authority and the Michigan Department of Transportation.

It all started with The Ariel in 1923. It was originally a river boat which had operated in the Detroit river. The Ariel, which accommodated only 20 cars, went out of service at the end of the 1923 season.

In the summer of 1924, the Highway Department expanded the fleet by purchasing two boats from the federal government— "The Colonel Pond" and " The Colonel Card" . The boats were lengthened from 130 feet to 180 feet so they could carry 40 cars each. One was renamed the "Sainte Ignace."

1924: MACKINAW CITY

The other boat purchased from the federal government was renamed " Mackinaw City." Business at the Straits nearly quadrupled in the second year, with more than 38,000 vehicles making the crossing. In 1925, the capacity of both boats increased to 60 cars each.

1928: The Straits of Mackinac

A third boat, " The Straits of Mackinac," joined the fleet in 1928 and provided service across the Straits until the opening of the Mackinac Bridge on November 1, 1957. This boat was built to carry approximately 35 vehicles. Within two years, the ferry was modified with an upper-level loading area, which increased the capacity to 90 cars and up to 400 passengers. For many years, " The Straits of Mackinac" was considered the flagship of the ferry fleet.

The Sainte Marie

In 1931, the Highway Department arranged with the Mackinac Transportation Company to carry cars across the Straits on a railroad icebreaker during the cold months. This arrangement turned out to be poor business for the State. So in 1936, the Highway Department leased the railroad icebreaker " Sainte Marie" for winter operations.

The ferry business continued to grow. In 1937, the Highway Department bought a converted Lake Michigan railway car ferry to provide additional service. The vessel was renamed the " City of Cheboygan." It had a capacity of 85 vehicles.

In 1938, another rebuilt railway car ferry was purchased. The " City of Munising" could carry 105 vehicles each trip across the Straits.

When the government purchased the " Mackinaw City" and the " Sainte Ignace" in 1940 for war, the State obtained a Pere Marquette Railway boat for service at the Straits of Mackinac. The ferry was renamed the " City of Petoskey." The vessel could carry 105 vehicles.

In the winter of 1952, the Highway Department acquired the 10,000 horsepower " Vacationland." Built by the Great Lakes Engineering Works in River Rouge, Michigan, it cost $4,745,000 and with a 75-foot beam and a 360 foot length, became the queen of the fleet. The " Vacationland" carried nearly 150 cars and trucks. The five-vessel fleet had a total carrying capacity of about 500 vehicles.

It was a great time and a great era in our State's history, and of course that of the Upper Peninsula. The last ferry operated by the Michigan State Ferry System was the City of Petoskey. She made her final voyage on November 1, 1957, marking the end of the state-operated ferry service. Over 30 million passengers and over 12 million cars used this system safely, impacting the economies of the communities in their respective Peninsulas. That's signif-icant, and it's how we lived. But I will never forget the lineups waiting our turn to board the ship.

CHAPTER 2

The Land Bridges

SAULT STE. MARIE INTERNATIONAL RAILROAD BRIDGE

The Sault Ste. Marie Railroad Bridge (our Jackknife bridge) was originally built in 1887, 1913, and 1959. It is owned by the Canadian National Railroad . It was built to facilitate rail traffic crossing St. Mary's River and the international border between Sault Ste. Marie, Michigan and Sault Ste. Marie, Ontario. It runs parallel to the Sault Ste. Marie International Bridge. The bridge was highly anticipated to act as a catalyst for commercial and industrial Development. There were years in the 1890s to the early 1900s that the economies were booming, agriculture was very strong, and lumber was still cut and shipped.

The bridge has nine Camelback spans and carries a single line of track. It is Michigan's most significant railroad bridge from an engineering historical standpoint and is eligible for listing in the National Registry of Historic Places.

Sault Ste. Marie International Railroad Bridge. There are several local stories about our "Jackknife Bridge ." The one story that many still chat about today was in the 20s and 30s, as the bridge was down, the locals used to walk across the bridge to visit family and girlfriends. My Uncle Glen was one of those characters, and he would drive his mother, my grandmother, as angry as could be at her older son. My Mother too, who he loved dearly, was his little sister. Mother didn't enjoy Uncle Glen telling his nephews about his crazy pranks. I guess she feared one of her two sons may try it himself. Mom would go as far as to tell us our uncle is lying to us. He would just wink at us and assured us he did it several times to visit Aunt Elma before he married her. She lived in Soo Canada.

The Railroad Bridge runs parallel to the highway
bridge and is the bridge on the left in the image.

The International Railroad Bridge is a magnificent landmark bridge whose significant size comes from a large number of smaller spans, rather than a single large bridge. Historically, the bridge is unmatched in its variety of span types. It is one of the few bridges in North America to have more than one type of movable span.

It is one of the few bridges in North America to have more than one type of movable span. Indeed, within this bridge, each of the three most common movable bridge types is represented. When all these sections are combined, the result is a bridge that is unrivaled in variety, size, beauty, and history. The structures that carry the railroad over the St. Mary's River and its canal systems are collectively referred to as the International Railroad Bridge. The bridge was designed for and continues to carry a single set of tracks. In addition to the variety of span types, the bridge's existing spans were also constructed at different times. Two dates are the most significant in the bridge's history. First, is 1887, which is what the oldest spans on this bridge date to, including the fixed camelback spans and the swing bridge. The second most significant date is 1913 when the Strauss Bascule Bridge Company designed the largest (and one of the most unusual) bascule span in the world for this bridge. Because of the variety of span types and span ages, photo galleries for this bridge as well as the narratives have all been organized into separate sections by bridge span type.

The bridge crosses the river and canals of St. Mary's River by making use of islands, some of which are artificial islands created by the locks. As such, from a technical definition, this bridge could be thought of as several bridges, since there are a few short sections that have track running along the ground.

The roughly estimated overall length of the bridge from end to end, including island sections, is 5,580 feet (1,700.8 meters). The bridge itself is utterly magnificent and is composed of an impressive nine spans! Each span is ten panels. The bridge is significant for its early construction date of 1887. The bridge was built by the Dominion Bridge Company of Lachine, Quebec.

SAULT INTERNATIONAL BRIDGE

We, in the Sault that followed the day-by-day construction of the bridge, were elated when it finally was completed. Sure, the ferries were our tradition, but the excitement of having our own bridge to Canada was so very strong. Many of our citizens, like we did with the Mackinac Bridge opening, lined up at the bridge plaza during the first week's opening to take our inaugural trip across, it was wonderful!

The Sault Ste. Marie International Bridge spans the St. Mary's River between the United States and Canada, connecting the twin cities Sault, Michigan and Sault, Ontario. The bridge is operated by the International Bridge Administration under the direction of the Sault Ste. Marie Bridge Authority, a binational governing body consisting of four directors appointed by the Governor of Michigan and four appointed by the Canadian govern-ment-owned Federal Bridge Corporation.

Here are the characteristics of the bridge: it is a Truss Arch Bridge design with a total length of 2.8 miles. Its width is 28 feet, with its longest span of 132 m and a clearance below 124 feet or 38 meters.

In 1954 the state of Michigan created the International Bridge Authority. [10] Canada followed in 1955, creating the St. Mary's River Co. The bridge was opened in 1962.

It has been a great success and has had a great impact on the economy of our two countries, but the immediate benefactors have been the twin cities of Sault Ste. Marie. It carries on average 7,000 cars per day, with the peak being 10,000 cars daily. The 100 millionth crossing occurred on March 1, 2018.

THE MACKINAC BRIDGE

The Mackinac Bridge, also referred to as the Mighty Mac, or Big Mac, is a suspension bridge that connects the Upper and Lower Peninsulas of the U.S. state of Michigan. It spans the Straits of Mackinac and the body of water connecting Lake Michigan and Lake Huron, two of the Great Lakes, our Inland Sea. Opened in 1957, the 26,372-foot-long (4.995 mi; 8.038

km) bridge is the world's 27th largest, and is the longest suspension bridge between anchorages in the Western Hemisphere. The Mackinac Bridge is part of the Interstate Highway System, which also includes the Lake Michigan and Huron components of the Great Lakes Circle. The bridge connects the city of St. Ignace to the north with the village of Mackinaw City to the south.

STATE OF MICHIGAN

The Bridge itself was opened on November 1, 1957. Its characteristics are quite unique as it crosses the Straits of Mackinac, approximately 5 miles across from Mackinac City to St. Ignace. Its daily use averages 11,600 vehicles that cross over. Of special significance is the Tower's height of 562 feet, making the bridge an impressive sight, even from afar, and perfect for great photos. The bridge's deck sits 200 feet above the water and was designed by David Steinman.

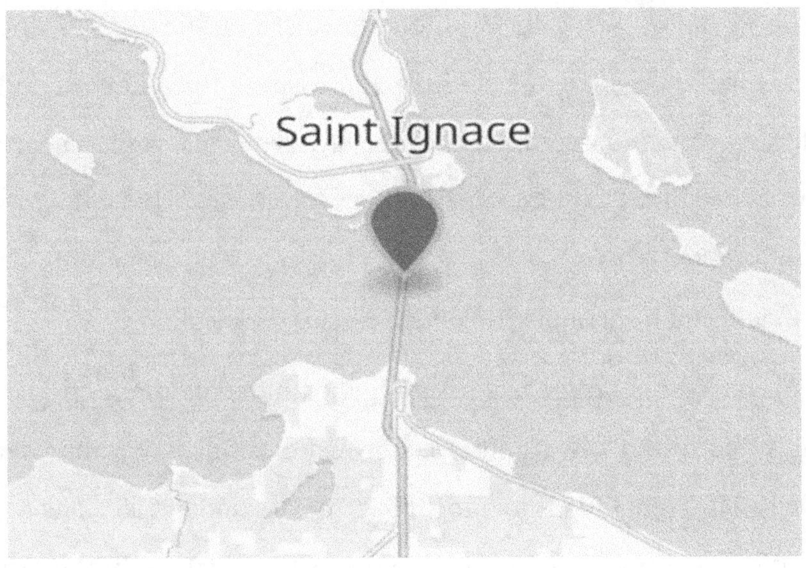

THE PORTAGE LAKE LIFT BRIDGE

The Portage Lake Lift Bridge connects the cities of Hancock and Houghton, in the US state of Michigan. It crosses Portage Lake, a portion of the waterway which cuts across the Keweenaw Peninsula, with a canal linking the final several miles to Lake Superior to the northwest. US Highway 41 and M-26 both routed across the bridge. It is the only land-based link between the north and south sections of the Keweenaw peninsula.

This moveable bridge is a lift bridge, with the middle section capable of being lifted from its low point of four feet clearance over the water to a clearance of 100 feet (30 m) to allow boats to pass underneath. The bridge is the world's heaviest and widest double-decked vertical-lift bridge.[6] More than 35,000 tons of concrete and 7,000 tons of steel went into the bridge, which replaced the narrow 54-year-old swing bridge, declared a menace to navigation on the busy Keweenaw Waterway. Hancock and Houghton hold an annual celebration called Bridgefest to commemorate the opening of the bridge which united their two communities.

THE INTERSTATE BRIDGE

The Interstate Bridge between Marinette, Wisconsin, and Menominee, Michigan, carries U.S. 41 over the Menominee River. The current bridge was completed in November 2005 and replaced the previous span built in 1929. The bridge it replaced, the Interstate Bridge, was built in 1929 for $700,000 (equivalent to $5.4 million in 2022 to carry US 41 over the Menominee River to the state line. This bridge replaced a series of bridges built to connect Marinette, Wisconsin and Menominee, Michigan across the river. The first bridge was built in 1865 with a second built in 1872. A drawbridge was built in 1897 that connected the two communities farther upstream between downtown Marinette and Menominee's Frenchtown neighborhood near what is now 19th Street. The first Interstate Bridge replaced the previous bridges. This bridge served as a vital connection between the two communities across the river. Residents of Menominee that worked in Marinette would drive as many as four times a day across the bridge in the 1930s and 1940s when families owned a single car. The bridge opened in December 1929, just months after the market crash of 1929.

THE ASHMUN STREET BRIDGE

Picture of Ashmun Street Bridge

Sault Ste. Marie, Michigan is a city of bridges. Each passes over our Canal and comes into our Island community. They are located on Portage, Spruce, Johnston, Bingham, Ashmun, and Fort Street. It certainly is a city with an unusually high number of unusual steel bridges. With its massive members, but unusually short span length for its type, this steel arch bridge on Ashmun Street remains in excellent condition, maintained at its original Power Canal location. The Power Canal is aptly named, as its water flow is used for generating power. As a result of the unusual power-generating and high velocity nature of the canal, none of the bridges over the canal were built with support in the water. This resulted in some bridge designs that ended up being unusual, much like our bridge on Ashmun Street. The Ashmun Street Bridge is a single span steel arch bridge. Steel arch bridges are a fairly uncommon structure type and are downright rare in Michigan. Nationwide, most steel through arch bridges tend to be used for long span crossings, often at a high level for navigational use. The Ashmun Street Bridge's span length of 257 feet, too long for the steel stringer bridges that Michigan commonly built during this period, is in contrast short compared to other steel through arch bridges in the country. The bridge according to the original plans was designed to function as a three-hinge arch for dead loads and a two-hinge arch for live loads.

With its unusual, and graceful through arch design, this bridge is extremely pleasing on an aesthetic level. Perhaps this bridge type was selected over other common bridge types that might be expected to be seen in a span length like this, like a steel truss bridge, for aesthetic reasons. It is also possible that the structure type was selected because of ease of construction over the Power Canal. It is possible that this arch bridge was constructed using the cantilever method, or by using backstays.

Both solutions would have prevented the need for falsework in the canal. In contrast, constructing a metal truss bridge over the canal might have been harder to do without putting falsework in the river during construction.

A plaque is present on the bridge, which identifies that the bridge was built in 1935, by Fry and Kain Inc, and Robert Hudson. The bridge was built jointly by the state of Michigan and the federal government. The plaque also mentions that the bridge was built with the cooperation of the Michigan Northern Power Company, most likely because the canal was the property of the power company.

Between the two arch lines, it carries two lanes and a left turn lane. Cantilevered sidewalks are present on both sides outside the arches.

Like the poem I Knew This Place by David Mallett. Well, I knew Ashmun Street Bridge, and I knew it very well, every sound and every smell. Since I was a child of 7, hitching a ride on the local Soo Line spur train that came right by our house, my cousins and I knew it was time to jump off at the Ashmun Bridge crossing. In a special way, the Ashmun Bridge became our point of no return. In other words,, "We get off the train now," or, we had a good long walk getting home. Going any further, we would be heading for trouble. That was always why Ashmun Street Bridge had something special about it, even as it was daily, we always crossed the Portage Street and Spruce Street bridges walking home from the theater, the gym, and school.

OUR ICE BRIDGES

We have at least two well-known Ice Bridges used quite often in the Winter, connecting Drummond Island with St. Joseph's Island, Ontario, Canada, and another used for years, the ice bridge connecting St. Ignace with Mackinac Island.

Ice bridge between Michigan's U.P., Canada open to snowmobilers. There is a more exciting, temporary way to travel between Michigan's Upper Peninsula and Canada each winter season —although modes of transportation are limited, and you still have to check in with customs.

An ice bridge forms between Drummond Island in Chippewa County and St. Joseph Island in Ontario, Canada during the winter months each year. Once the ice has frozen to a safe depth, locals are able to enjoy winter activities on the trails.

The Drummond Island ice bridge between Michigan and Canada is now open for snowmobilers who are feeling adventurous and want to ping-pong between the two countries.

As of Monday, Feb. 13, the ice between Drummond and St. Joseph islands has been deemed thick enough for safe travel between Drummond Island and St. Joseph Island, Ontario, U.S. Customs and Border Protection (CBP) announced. It will remain open until the ice degrades and becomes hazardous in the spring.

In addition to snowmobiles, aero sleighs, dog sleds, bicycles, cross-country skis and snowshoes are permitted on the ice bridge, but cars and trucks are not allowed.

Canadians and Drummond Islanders have planted a line of small pine trees in the ice between the two islands to guide travelers across the 12-mile ice bridge.

It's been a proven way to promote international tourism, and it works.

MACKINAC ISLAND ICE BRIDGE

Big Mac is easily one of Michigan's most famous bridges, but do you know about Mackinac Island's other, lesser-known bridge? The "Ice Bridge" is a natural pathway to Mackinac Island that forms each winter, as long as the conditions are right.

If the wind is calm and the temperatures dip below zero for enough nights in a row, a solid plane of ice forms on the waters of Lake Michigan. Each year, locals organize a path on this ice stretching from St. Ignace to Mackinac Island.

Generally, the bridge is at its strongest — and therefore safest — somewhere between January and February. However, it's always best practice to consult the local coast guard, fire department, and meteorologists to get a good idea of how safe the ice is before your trip.

The ice bridge today is nearly 5 miles in length. It goes back many years in the history of Mackinac Island. Hundreds of years ago, the British used this same ice bridge to haul men and materials across the ice as they moved Fort Michilimackinac from the mainland to the island. In the 1800s, dog sleds brought weekly mail, and horse-drawn cutters hauled firewood on this stretch of ice. Today, locals and out-of-town adventurers take their snowmobiles, cross the ice bridge and it's quite a cool adventure. I did it once in the 1980s, and it truly was unbelievable to see Mackinac Island from a completely different viewpoint than I ever had seen before. It really was a once-in-a-lifetime event to ride on a sled and see the island like this. I've been on the Island a few times in the summer, and what is normally green, lush, and a fun, unique location, turned into this beautiful winter wonderland."

Have you traveled across the ice bridge or visited
Mackinac Island in the winter?

CHAPTER 3

Harness Racing In The Up

Our Dad just loved harness racing and used to take my brother John and me to Sault, Canada and take in the standardbred racing circuit, which was quite popular in the Sault from the 1930s to the 1970s.

It's another name for Harness Racing. What was so much fun however was listening to Dad tell his story as a driver (not jockey) of trained horses pulling a sulky, for his father's cousin, Frank Gillespie. The Gillespie's came in from Canada as well from Ireland near Sligo, and married as John T McCarthy did, to marry one of the Cox family twins. My great-grandfather married Susannah, and Frank Gillespie married her twin sister Bridget Cox, a fiery redhead. Both families settled in the Tone area, a few miles outside Pickford. Well, Frank Jr. loved working with his hands and was a fairly successful builder . He loved horses, especially the Trotters and Pacers. His father kept some trotters, as he grew up a young boy in Canada. When Dad was 14, Frank taught him the ropes of being a driver for the harness circuit. My father loved it. He had a lot to learn, just the basics, before he was taught how to drive the horse.

Almost all North American races are at a distance of one mile (1,609 m). Most races are run on tracks constructed solely for harness racing (some with banked turns), but a few tracks did conduct both harness and thoroughbred flat racing. Frank used to take his three horses to a race, and off he drove with dad to the county fairs. They then would go and enter a horse into the various races. Oftentimes they would race in Soo, Canada.

HARNESS RACING IN ONTARIO

Though the vast majority of races are one mile, races are contested on several different sized tracks. Dad always watched closely the distance, as most common distances were 1/2-mile, 5/8 mile, and 1- mile tracks. He knew two of Frank's horses liked the longer distances, while Dad himself loved the 5/8-mile track. He would say, with a lot of pride, he knew his horse, Danny Boy. Danny Boy did much better on the smaller tracks because there were fewer turns. Frank taught Dad to hold tight the reins as Danny Boy's Driver on the shorter track because early speed was important, and he needed to let Danny Boy set his quickest trotting pace right away. Different from the longer stretch of 1 mile, which favors horses with late speed, ideal for a come from behind racing win. The shorter run was geared to a very fast and immediate, stronger pace that normally wins. My Father loved it, and he would say driving Danny Boy was just beautiful, and "he made us money. "

Dad would make us walk round the track, and he asked permission to go to the stables. Dad was wanting to place a bet. He wanted to see some of the horses who would be racing. Of course, the people managing the operation were suspicious of us. But Dad assured them all by telling them he had over 150 races under his belt as a driver when he was a teenager, and he wanted to show his boys the beauty of these horses. They seemed to understand and walked around with us to see some of the horses before they ran.

Dad would be telling us all stories as we were walking through the stables. He wanted to look at the faces of the horses, their mains, and their legs. He would tell us and the guide helping us in the stables, when the race starts, most drivers will contend for the lead right away from the gate. "They then try to avoid getting ' boxed in' as the horses form into two lines— one on the rail and the other outside."

With Danny Boy, he liked riding the rail behind the leader. It was a choice spot he said, known as the "pocket", and in that position is said to have a "garden trip" . Third on the rail is an undesirable spot, known on small tracks as the "death hole" . John and I used to get a kick out of Dad remembering the terms used as a driver, and how much he really knew about Harness racing . He loved horses and truly thought Harness racing was the very best. As we were walking out of the stables, a certain horse caught his eye, and right away he was determined to place a bet on him. He would tell us, now watch for this horse at the finish, watch how he breaks and digs in. The finish of the race is always close and exciting. Every trip we made those few years going to Canada and taking in the Harness racing, we really did win some money.

CHAPTER 4

Sawmills Of The EUP

By 1902, our Power Plant of hydroelectric power, which had been under construction since 1898, was now operational, and heavy Industry began to come to the Sault. Our economy, in those early years of the 1900s, was becoming agriculture based. But our EUP region had several sawmills of varying sizes that supplied a number of jobs to its residents and citizens. Sawmills in the Sault, Newberry, Engadine, Manistique, Brevort Lake, Shelldrake, Eckerman, Naubinway, Trout Lake, Curtis, Rudyard, Kinross, Pickford, DeTour, Dafter, Raber, RACO, and Dollarville provided a nice financial bounce to the economy. But then, there were the bigs—the huge employers—very large companies with significant impact on the regional economy. These were the big companies in Seney and Grand Marais, the Richardson and Avery Company outside Brimley and the Cadillac Lumber company in Sault Ste Marie.

Boom Logs towed through 4th lock, 1920s, Soo Locks.

Chippewa County Logs

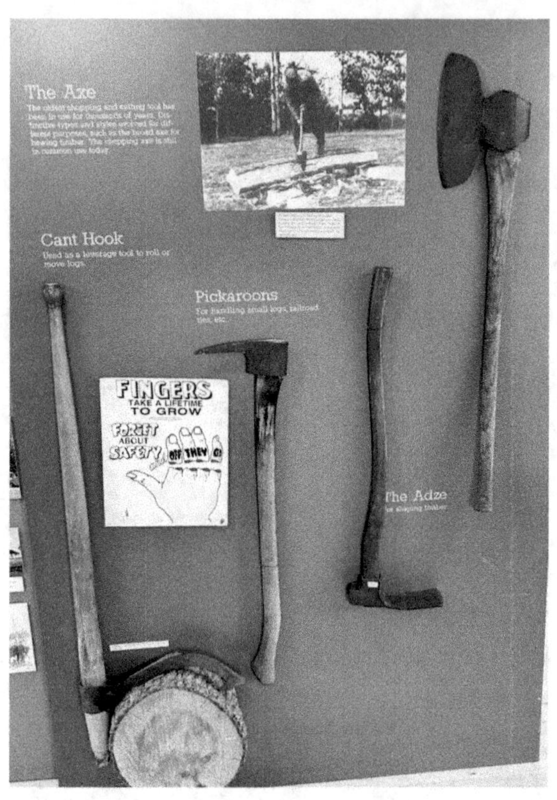

Logging Tools used at Barrett Logging Company, In Newberry.

SAWS USED AT THE CAMP.

I've mentioned my grandfather several times, we all called Pop. Well, he was a true lumberjack. I loved his stories, all my brothers and sisters did. I loved his songs, and I really loved his tales of the logging camps in Seney and Grand Marais where he worked for nearly 5 years. I always asked him how the lumberjacks lived, what they ate, and how long they worked each day. Furthermore, I always heard how tough they were and how they enjoyed a good fight. I had to ask him, did he have fun fighting? My mother would just say, " Dad, you don't need to answer that."

Lumberjack Breakfast, courtesy of the Logging Museum

Between Pop and Dad, we kids got our own picture. However, the fighting was less about getting even, than it was for the sheer delight of it. Pop would just say, "It was fun." There was never a problem with guns and knives, most of the time, but even the toughest of the loggers would gouge your eyes and bite your ears. Pop and Dad also said, while we were listening closely, sometimes a logger would stomp on his opponent in his nail studded "calked boots." This move, they called it, was, "putting the boots to him" and it usually left your opponent in a bad way. Pop would finish, "now you boys don't need to act this way. We were just loggers, and you had to be rough, tough, and hard to bluff ." John and I had a good hard laugh hearing that.

Pop was never one to complain, but he would say he didn't like the sleeping conditions at the camps as he would work 12–14 hours a day, in all kinds of weather. He said he was always tired and hungry, but he was always warm in the camp. There was a 5-foot wood stove right in the middle of the camp where the loggers lived, and it gave out great heat. He loved their breakfasts. However, he said, "It was worth every pain he lived through."

The Allen Lumber Mill, Barbeau, MI

Kinross Logging Camp

Logging near Donaldson, 1898

As I began my research on life in those camps, it was very apparent that Life was never luxurious in the logging camps of Michigan's Upper Peninsula including Ontonagon, Seney, and Grand Marais regions. Rough roads chopped out of the forest led to the hastily constructed log buildings of the camp, which might house up to 150 men. It was a true part of their legendary reputation— as I said earlier, Lumberjacks were renowned for their toughness and strength. My Dad talked of a headstone in Seney's Boot Hill Cemetery he saw, that simply states, " Died fighten." And I asked Pop if this was true, he just smiled and laughed. Dad had to say what he knew, and Pop just smiled again. Pop did know something he heard of what happened in Seney about the man who shot President McKinley. Pop couldn't pronounce his name, but Dad knew the story and would tell it. The man's name was Leon Czolgosz, a Michigan born son of Polish immigrants. Czolgosz was said to have been employed for a time by the Manistique Railroad on the section crew at Beaver Junction, ten miles south of Grand Marais. After he left Seney, he became radicalized by anarchist speeches and propaganda. His travels eventually led him to Buffalo, New York, where on September 6, 1901, he shot President William McKinley, who was greeting guests at the Pan-American Exposition. McKinley died of his wounds eight days later.

Pop enjoyed his short stay in Grand Marais, however.

Grand Marais in the early 1900s was a town dependent on the lumber and fishing industries. Many of these houses were brought up from Seney, 25 miles to the south, when the lumber boom played out there and moved north to Grand Marais. He worked there during the winter of 1914- 1915.

Grand Marais was a lumber boomtown at one point, and several sawmills dotted the shores of Grand Marais Bay. The Cook, Curtis, and Miller sawmill was one of the largest, and stood on the south side of the bay. This was the mill where Pop had worked.

This photo, provided by the Michigan Department of Natural Resources, shows a Tahquamenon log jam during the era at the turn of the century.

Log Jam at Tahquamenon Falls

Did you ever hear of Lumberjills ?

I first heard Pop mention this, and at first, I couldn't believe it. It was common for the use of this word in the lumber camps of women and children working mainly in the kitchens. My cousin Eva Hassett and her mother, my great-aunt Hattie, every summer worked in the camps in Rudyard and Kinross. Even though logging was by and large a male-centric industry, there were women present on campsites. Many of these women were typically wives/daughters/relatives of the foremen, and they worked as either cooks or cleaners. There never has been any proof that women actually worked in hard labor of logging or in the sawmill, but during WWII in England women were called Lumberjills and could be found doing hard labor.

Lumberjills—It looks as though she is carrying a firework through a city street. Regardless, I seriously hope that using people as pack mules was not that common. But, maybe.

Life was challenging, especially during wintertime. There was no lack of snow come winter. Early residents turned to shovels and horse-drawn plows, but the railroad had a better idea: a plow train.

Grand Marais Historical Society Photo

This plow train ran along tracks that led from Seney to Grand Marais. In the winter, residents depended on the train as their link to the outside world. When he finally came home and re-joined his brothers at their mill, Pop had to take the train to Seney and head north to the Sault on their train. Roads for transport were worse than poor.

The pine grew primarily as pure stands, on sandy, dry soils in the northern 2/3 of the state.

North of an imaginary line from Muskegon and Saginaw, the pines grew: white, jack and red, as well as other conifers. It was the white pine that allowed the heyday of the lumber industry. Many white pines were over 200 years old, 200 feet in height and five feet in diameter. Michigan's pine became important as the supply of trees in the northeast was used. By 1880, Michigan was producing as much lumber as the next three states combined.

SOME OF THE LARGER MILLS

Richardson & Avery Company

Six investors formed Richardson & Avery Company, which harvested and sold various types of hardwood to businesses in Michigan and Wisconsin. The town of RACO (named from the initials of the company) was established after the company built a sawmill in 1913. In 1914, six men pooled their resources and bought about 36,000 acres of timber land in north central Chippewa County, MI for the purpose of manufacturing lumber. These investors, Sewell L. Avery, Waldo A. Avery, Howard C. Richardson, Robert K. Richardson, Ard E. Richardson, and Lloyd M. Richardson formed the Richardson & Avery Company, which created the town of RACO to serve as its headquarters.

For nearly two decades, this firm harvested and sold various types of hardwoods to businesses in Michigan and Wisconsin, creating in the process an enterprise valued at over a million dollars, and employed over 150 men.

As the concern grew, it became dependent upon greater sources of supply and markets. To meet these needs, Richardson & Avery Company merged in November 1930 with the Cadillac Lumber & Chemical Company, establishing the Cadillac-Soo Lumber Company based in Sault Ste. Marie, Michigan.

Aerial view of the Cadillac-Soo Plant

The Cadillac-Soo Lumber Company

As I mentioned earlier, in 1930, the company merged with Raco Land & Timber Company, and Richardson-Avery Company to become the Cadillac-Soo Lumber Company. After the merger in 1930, the company was worth $5 million and owned 155,000 acres of forest land from Raco west along the south shore of Lake Superior. A Baldwin steam locomotive, believed to be the last used in Michigan logging, ran from these woodlands to the mill, which was located in a part of town called Algonquin, off West Easterday Avenue. The mill was capable of producing about 63,000 (board) feet of hardwood lumber, or 100,000 feet of softwood lumber per nine-hour shift. It was said to be the largest sawmill east of the Mississippi in the 1950s. The Cadillac-Soo Lumber Company remained a principal business in the Sault until its closure was announced on April 30, 1956. At the time of its closure, the company employed 154. Some offers for sale were considered by the company, but the board of directors opted to close the mill. The plant became inefficient compared to newer mills, and the timber that remained nearby did not justify the investment that would have been required to modernize it. The site is now occupied by the industrial incubator operated by the city and Lake Superior State University.

The Cadillac-Soo Lumber Company was huge and employed hundreds at the mill and kept loggers very busy. They really became a trademark of the Sault community and remained so for many years.

School Songs From The Sault

One of the greatest stories ever told growing up was about a little man named Felix 'Butsie' Tavern. I even had the privilege of seeing it unfold before my own eyes, while I was in my school years. He would run out onto the floor of a b-ball game at half-time or run to the team's side in a football game. Even at the age of 80, he would skate to the middle of an ice rink between periods in a hockey game.

Every time he does, Butsie would be wearing the varsity jacket or sweater of the respective school. He then led the crowd to sing some cheers for the team, and oftentimes led in the singing of the school's alma mater or fight song. It was an amazing story, and even more amazing to watch firsthand. A small man with a very powerful voice, and with a heart of gold. His passion and his love for sports ran second to his love for the kids playing in our communities . He knew something back then that very few of us knew or understood, but his contribution should never be forgotten. Citizens like Butsie, are among us today, and they help build a better community, and that is exactly what Felix 'Butsie' Tavern did. And he did it for years, right up through his eighties. He knew school anthems and sang them. They were important then, and they still are today.

They were equally important in my high school years as they are today. A school anthem is always sung to enhance the sense of dedication and belonging towards one's alma mater . Hence, it creates a sense of loyalty and devotion in the minds of the students. Schools are places where groups of young people gather with a purpose and an intent that speaks of the hope they are offering for the future and for our world. And besides, it makes our parents proud too, and happy for their children to go to that school.

Let us sing this from the rooftops.

At Sault High and Loretto Catholic, our school songs were obvious — we were committing to treading the way to freedom and truth, doing our best, and making a difference in the world.

Schools are places where groups of young people gather with a purpose and an intent that speaks of the hope they are offering for the future and for our world.

Let us sing this from the rooftops.

Sault High School Victory Song

We are out for victory,

We are out to win, team,

So let's have a cheer from everyone here

Earl V. Moore, former Dean of the School of Music at University of Michigan was the composer of the Sault High Fight Song, in Sault Ste Marie, Michigan. Also, the composer of the University of Michigan's alternative fight song "Varsity". The fight song's lyrics will never be forgotten. My sincere thanks to Nancy Andary for digging out this information.

Loretto School Song

Loretto, fight for a victory fight for the crowd

Give us a victory as we shout so loud

Loretto, go go go, with banners flying on high

Fight fight fight for Alma Mater we cry

Rah Rah Rah

Loyal and true we stand Faithful are we

Cheering our blue and white to victory

Angels we're out to win

By Mary Wood

Years after I graduated from Loretto, I asked Mary Wood who wrote the School Song for Loretto, what prompted her to write the lyrics, and the music to a great song. Her response was 100% Mary Wood if you knew her. She said simply, "We didn't have one, so I asked the folks in charge at Loretto to take some action. It's my Alma Mater, too. And I'm sick, sore, and tired of staying quiet, and it's time we have our own song. "

The rest is all about our history in the Sault community, and the history of hundreds of graduates passing through the halls of Loretto.

The very same for our graduates from Sault High, with its great history and great traditions. We just need to look at our leaders of today, and we know what our schools have provided for our community's best interest.

CHAPTER 6

Sports Teams
From The Sault

Before my dear friend Donald Paul Byron passed, he came to our 50th year class reunion of Loretto High School in Sault, Michigan. We had many hours of chats, just catching up, and asking one another, do you remember this? Do you remember that? We were neighbors, growing up as grade schoolers, and on through High School. He and his family lived just around the block on Spruce Street in our East End. Our mothers, too, were classmates and teammates on their basketball team when Loretto was an all-girls school. He was a brilliant storyteller, and anyone who knew him, knew full well he believed in detail, he believed in the truth, and he believed in verifiable facts. In other words, there was no Blarney. When he got to his story, it was truth, not fiction. When he was young, he was known to us simply as BYREE. It stuck with him all of his life, but his name was Donald Paul, and he went by Paul. One of his great interests and passions was always the Soo sports teams. So, as he aged, he undertook hours of research with the Soo Evening News archives and began his statistical analysis of the Soo Sports teams from the years 1945-1970. He chose this period of time, as Loretto existed as a Co-Ed high school from 1945-70 before it was closed. So, he studied the very best of the best of our football and basketball high school teams at both Sault High and Loretto.

After the reunion, he wanted me to come over to his house, and we spoke for three hours about his findings. He had papers with his notes on statistical achievements of the various individual players who starred on those teams. He had the school season records of each team. In the early days before the 1960s at Loretto they played with Class D school teams, it was all based-on school population, so they did not play 11 men football. But after 1960 they did, and the smaller village schools stepped up as well. The Great Lakes Conference, and the EUP Athletic Conference, were homes to the Sault High Blue Devils and the Loretto Angels for those years. Over the history of the conferences, there were some fairly strong teams and individual achievement. In other words, some elite players came from these conferences, with all state recognition and college scholarships offered for their accomplishments, Sault High and Loretto shared in those awards.

As I said earlier, Paul was a fine storyteller, really one of the best I've heard. He just loved individual accomplishment and had at the tip of his tongue the football leaders in points, rushing yards, touchdowns, receiving yards, interceptions, recovered fumbles. In basketball, he knew the leaders in points per game average, rebounds, steals, free throws made, and he even knew how many technical fouls a team has had. I found that statistic very interesting, but Paul maintained it was crucial.

What he surmised with his data gathering and research was the best of the best, and in his sure way, here they were:

The Sault High 1956 football team was top shelf. A conference winner and highly rated School in the State. Its players and team record received statewide recognition, and players became leaders in the community. They became local town heroes as time lapsed.

He continued with the 1959 Sault High basketball team, which was also an elite team. They were conference champions and statewide leaders. They were coached by one of the very best creative coaches ever, and a team of players who brought pride to the community and accolades from both the UP and State. That team is still spoken of today, but equal mention should be given to the 2012 team, although not part of Paul's research. Now to be fair we had some good teams at both Soo High and Loretto, and the 1951 and 1959 Basketball teams at Loretto should receive honorable mention.

But he drew the line with the 1963 football teams of Sault High and Loretto. They were the very best of the best for several reasons, he thought.

Yes, they were both the conference champions and both were highly rated within the state structure. Both teams saw individual stardom within their conference and throughout the UP and State. But according to Paul, for the very first time, both teams were undefeated at the same time. He was so proud of that fact, he said,, "Mike, think of that, never, ever before, have both our high school teams ever gone undefeated together." "That's historic, man, I love it."

One of our greatest stars was Sault High's own Dennis Porter, named the best in the UP in 1963. Sault High was just one of four teams in the UP to go undefeated that year. Loretto was the second team.

Named Best In U. P.

3 All-U.P. Grid Teams

Class A-B Selections

First Team

Name	School
Dennis Porter	Sault High
Dale Horschner	Escanaba
Tom Domres	Gladstone
Jerry Lackey	Sault High
Bill Bassett	Ironwood
Dick Burbey	Kingsford
Ron Tortelli	Kingsford
Frank Trotter	Escanaba H. N.
Dick Berlinski	Kingsford
Andy Benson	Sault High
Dan Schram	Gladstone

Second Team

Name	School
Tom Soli	Marquette
Eugene Fregotto	Escanaba H. N.
Dave Sharkus	Menominee
Paul Monette	Kingsford
Mike Smith	Iron River
Dave Sundberg	Calumet
Bob Pearson	Marquette
Roland Pakinen	Ironwood
Frank Verbos	Ironwood
Jim Dougovito	Stephenson
Don Mylchrest	Stambaugh

Class C-D Selections

FIRST TEAM

— Bill Duncan, Crystal Falls; Don Stipech, Houghton.
s — Jack Clark, Wakefield; Steve Burr, Norway.
s — Doug Madigan, Sault Loretto; John Kelly, Houghton.
r — Dick Sofio, Bessemer.
— Terry Salmk, Wakefield; Jack Spuhler, Sault Loretto;
inolfi, Wakefield; Ernie Brumbaugh, Norway.

SECOND TEAM

— Larry Makimaa, Ontonagon; Bob Perkins, Sault Loret-

es — Wes Wiggens, Crystal Falls; Lee Biekkola, Houghton.
ls — John Hayden, Crystal Falls; Loren Jakkola, Wake-

— John Fryxell, Houghton; John Torsky, Cedarville.
rs — Tom Landree, Ontonagon; Angelo Diqui, Crystal
l Bennetts, Bessemer.

cv

JACK SPUHLER

Now, I should have acknowledged the Loretto record, which Paul was correct in stating. The Loretto team of 1963 had an undefeated season, and that means no ties. But the UP Sports Bureau, the media group for the

State Athletic Association, someway and somehow had Loretto tie with St. Ignace by 13-13. Now Paul knew the final score was 33-13, for the team from Loretto, and he tried to make his CASE to the correct change to the State Athletic Association.

You can easily see how the error happened, just look at the score, but it wasn't 13-13, it was 33-13. But the change didn't happen. But Paul wasn't pleased, and he was pissed off. His appeal was not even heard. The state record had been left unchanged. It remains so to this very day. Now think of it this way. A record wrongfully stated 61 years ago, discovered by Paul, prompted him to spend hours researching data, reviewing scores, reviewing news and sports clippings, and every possible statistic. His dream was to present the whole CASE for reconsideration to the State of Michigan, and "get that damned thing changed." That was his passion.

I spoke with several members of that great Loretto team, and started with its quarterback, Tony Bosbous. Tony is a very interesting fellow, he's soft-spoken, but when he heard of the state's foolish error, the state was not willing to change it. He said bluntly, "That's all hogwash. We beat them badly. Let 's get that stupid thing changed." Tony is now retired from politics. But he is the longest elected Mayor of the City of Sault, Michigan, where he served for 18 years. Other team members I chatted with were Pete Campbell and Tim Kinney. They just echoed Tony with a similar tone and language. Pete dug out of the archives of the Sault News: The final victory of Loretto that year of the 1963 season. Loretto won and had an 8-0 record. Here is the headline on the Sports page of the Soo Evening News:

Soo Loretto Jolts Cheboygan To Cap Unbeaten Grid Season

Coach Bob McKerrol's Loretto Angels climaxed an undefeated football season Saturday night with their eighth straight win of the season, a thrilling 27-14 victory over strong Cheboygan Catholic Central.

Two touchdown efforts by halfbacks Jack Spuhler and Frank Groben led the Angels in the finale.

Spuhler's touchdowns gave him a season scoring mark of 147 points. Spuhler, U.P. scoring champ, tallied 23 touchdowns.

Spuhler's touchdowns came on a beautiful 67-yard run in the opening quarter, and a 99-yard run on a pass from quarterback Tony Bosbous.

Groben, who showed tremendous potential in the six games he played, scored on runs of 29 and 49 yards.

The Angels held a commanding 20-0 lead going into the second half of the game. But Cheboygan, a class C power, came back with single touchdowns in the third and fourth quarters, and ended another drive on the eight-yard line of the Angels. Loretto sewed the game up with its only touchdown of the second half, a 99-yard touchdown pass from Bosbous to Spuhler.

The game, viewed by a large crowd, watched the second Sault school climax an undefeated season. The Sault High Blue Devils, with an 8-0 record, finished their schedule last week.

Loretto opened the scoring at the 7:37 mark of the opening quarter. Spuhler, behind some fine blocking by Loretto's offensive line, broke loose and outraced Cheboygan's secondary and rambled 67 yards for a touchdown.

Perkins kicked the ball through the goal posts and Loretto had a 7-0 lead.

Loretto increased its lead to 13-0 in the final minutes of the first quarter after an exchange of fumbles. Loretto recovered the second one on the 35-yard line of Cheboygan. Groben spun loose for a 29-yard touchdown run.

Groben, Loretto's fleet-footed halfback, gave the Angels a 19-0 lead midway in the second quarter. After taking a Cheboygan punt on the Catholic Central 49 yard line, he broke around right end and sprinted 49 yards down the sidelines for a TD.

Spuhler hit Bosbous with the pass for the extra point and Loretto led 20-0 at the half.

Cheboygan came out after the half a new ball team. After taking the kick-off on its own 31, the downstaters marched 69 yards to the Loretto end-zone.

Larry Bucalos climaxed the drive by plunging the final three yards for the touchdown.

Tom Hungerford ran the extra point and the score was 20-7.

Cheboygan came back in the early minutes of the final quarter to score again. Charles Couture climaxed a 60-yard drive by hitting Bucalos with a 19-yard touchdown pass.

The conversion attempt was good and the score was 20-14.

Cheboygan had another golden opportunity to score minutes later. After taking the ball on the 50 yard line. Behind the power running of Ray Drake, Cheboygan moved the ball to the Loretto eight-yard line.

Dennis Fabry intercepted a stray Cheboygan aerial on the one-yard line to halt the drive at that point.

After trying two unsuccessful runs to move the ball away from his goal line, Bosbous found Spuhler all by himself behind the Cheboygan secondary and hit him with a pass which covered 99 yards for the clincher.

Tim Kinney, Jack Spuhler, Bob Perkins, Merle King and Rich Peller were standouts in the defensive line for the Angels.

Spuhler, the Upper Peninsula scoring champion, and Groben were the main offensive threats for Coach Bob McKerroll's championship football team.

Here is the first paragraph of the sports page, from the Sault Evening News. You read it and decide. It's very clear the record was 8-0, and a printing error was made of the actual record that was given to the state from its media bureau.

"Coach Bob McKerrol's Loretto Angels climaxed an undefeated football season Saturday night with their eighth straight win of the season, a thrilling 27-14 victory over strong Cheboygan Catholic Central."

And check this one: Sault Evening News, October 31, 1963.

The third paragraph is the most critical: "Loretto defeated Pickford, St. Ignace, DeTour, Engadine, Rudyard, Cedarville, Brimley and Cheboygan Catholic." Loretto was one of four undefeated football teams in the UP in the 1963 season!

Coach Bob McKerroll's undefeated Sault Loretto football team was the highest scoring eleven in Upper Peninsula football circles, with a season total of 32 points.

Loretto, one of four undefeated teams in the Upper Peninsula, rounded out its 1963 football schedule last Saturday night, with a 27-14 victory over Cheboygan Catholic Central.

Loretto defeated Pickford, St. Ignace, DeTour, Engadine, Rudyard, Cedarville, Brimley and Cheboygan Catholic Central on its road to a perfect football season.

Jack Spuhler, Loretto's outstanding halfback won the scoring championship in the Upper Peninsula with a season total of 147, based on 23 touchdowns and nine extra points.

Here were the State records: Sault High 8-0

GREAT LAKES CONFERENCE	CONFERENCE		
	W-L-T	AVE	PF-PA
Sault Ste. Marie Blue Devils	6-0-0	1.000	138-39
Escanaba Eskymos	5-1-0	.833	113-38
Munising Mustangs	4-2-0	.667	85-84
Gladstone Braves	3-2-1	.583	146-105
Marquette Redmen	3-2-1	.583	74-86
Manistique Emeralds	3-3-0	.500	76-60
Ishpeming Hematites	2-4-0	.333	65-67
Stephenson Eagles	2-4-0	.333	87-127
Newberry Indians	1-5-0	.167	73-144
Negaunee Miners	0-6-0	.000	45-152

CONFERENCE			ALL-GAMES		
W-L-T	AVE	PF-PA	W-L-T	AVE	PF-P
6-0-0	1.000	138-39	8-0-0	1.000	225-
5-1-0	.833	113-38	7-1-0	.875	147-
4-2-0	.667	85-84	5-3-0	.625	135-1
3-2-1	.583	146-105	5-2-1	.687	190-1
3-2-1	.583	74-86	3-4-1	.437	81-1
3-3-0	.500	76-60	4-4-0	.500	109-
2-4-0	.333	65-67	3-5-0	.375	77-
2-4-0	.333	87-127	2-6-0	.250	87-1
1-5-0	.167	73-144	3-5-0	.375	101-1
0-6-0	.000	45-152	1-7-0	.125	79-1

Major players receiving all conference and all state recognition were Dennis Porter, Andy Benson, Jerry Lackey, Peter Williamson, and Jody Kline.

State Records, Loretto 7-0-1

1963 Standings

EASTERN UPPER PENINSULA ATHLETIC CONF.	CONFERENCE			ALL-GAMES	
	W-L-T	AVE	PF-PA	W-L-T	AVE
Sault Ste. Marie Loretto Angels	5-0-0	1.000	210-51	7-0-1	.937
Cedarville Trojans	3-1-1	.700	90-70	4-1-1	.750
Pickford Panthers	3-2-0	.600	66-66	3-5-0	.375
Brimley Bays	2-3-0	.400	94-90	2-4-0	.333
DeTour Raiders	1-3-1	.300	33-57	2-3-1	.417
Engadine Eagles	0-5-0	.000	30-189	0-5-0	.000

ALL-GAMES

W-L-T	AVE	PF-PA
7-0-1	.937	301-78
4-1-1	.750	111-77
3-5-0	.375	84-134
2-4-0	.333	107-110
2-3-1	.417	53-70
0-5-0	.000	30-189

Major players of that undefeated Loretto team receiving Conference, and state recognition were Jack Spuhler, Frank Groben, Doug Madigan, Tony Bosbous, Merle King, Tim Kinney, Bob Perkins, and Rich Peller. Jack Spuhler was the UP-scoring champ that season with 23 touchdowns and 147 points. In fact, Jack averaged scoring 18 points per game—another U.P. record.

Paul's game-by-game research, going through evening News archives and Public Library filings. 1963 football Season with teams and scores— Loretto 8-0

1963 - Undefeated   ***
Win : Loretto - 14   Pickford   - 0
Win : Loretto - 33   St. Ignace   - 13
Win : Loretto - 24   DeTour   - 0
Win : Loretto - 77   Engadine   - 12
Win : Loretto - 51   Rudyard   - 0
Win : Loretto - 45   Cedarville   - 24
Win : Loretto - 50   Brimley   - 15
Win : Loretto - 27   Cheboygan Cath. - 14
*** Sault High Undefeated, Also !!

One final piece of important information from the St. Ignace Newspaper— check this one out.

Jack Spuhler Sparks Angels

Loretto Tramples Saints

ST. IGNACE — Sault Loretto Catholic, triggered by the offensive efforts of Jack Spuhler, defeated the St. Ignace Saints, 33-13 in a non-conference game played here last night.

Spuhler staked a tireless offensive show while picking up 145 yards in 14 rushing attempts, returned two kickoffs for 50 and 65 yards, and caught two key passes to set up the touchdowns.

Loretto opened the scoring in the first quarter when Tony Bosbous hit Pat Murphy with a 16-yard touchdown pass. Jack Spuhler's try for the extra point was wide and Loretto led 6-0.

Jimmy Spuhler increased the lead to 12-0 in the second quarter by going eight yards on a plunge. Jack Spuhler ran the extra point and Loretto pulled ahead 13-0.

St. Ignace came back cut Loretto's lead to 13-6, when Giz Brown scored on a quarterback sneak. The try for the extra point was wide and the score at the half was 13-6.

Loretto pushed its lead to 18-6 early in the third quarter on a 10 yard sweep by Jack Spuhler. Spuhler's run for the extra point was good and Loretto lead 19-6.

Loretto's lead increased to 25-6 on a quarterback sneak by Bosbous. The extra point was good and Loretto boosted its margin to 26-6.

Bill Fenlon scored St. Ignace's second and final touchdown on a three yard sweep to whittle Loretto's lead to 26-12. Dan O'Roark's try for the extra point was good.

Loretto scored its final touchdown with five minutes left in the game on a 24-yard pass play from Bosbous to Murphy.

Pat Murphy, Spuhler's running mate at the halfback position, picked up 92 yards in nine carries.

Jim Spuhler picked up 62 yards in 11 rushing attempts.

Bosbous hit on five of nine passes for 112 yards and two touchdowns.

Jack Spuhler, Merle King, Scott Baker, Bob Perkins, Doug Madigan and Rich Peller were defensive standouts for Loretto.

Loretto will move back in the conference wars next week when they meet the DeTour Red Raiders in a home attraction.

St. Ignace will travel to Petoskey to meet St. Francis in a Straits-Huron Conference game next Friday.

NFL Kickoff

Pick Dallas Over Cards

By BOB GREEN

Associated Press Sports Writer

The Dallas Cowboys, with the town to themselves and talking title, open the National Football League's 44th season tonight against St. Louis' crippled Cardinals.

An hour or so later the Detroit Lions rumble onto the field against the Rams in Los Angeles. The rest of the league swings into action in five games Sunday afternoon.

Dallas and Detroit are favored in the openers, the improving Cowboys by a touchdown and the tough Lions by two.

The Cowboys, the only pro team in town since the Texans moved their American Football League

THE STANDINGS

By THE ASSOCIATED PRESS

National League

	W.	L.	Pct.	G.B.
Los Angeles	90	58	.608	—
St. Louis	88	61	.591	2½
Milwaukee	80	68	.541	19
San Francisco	79	69	.534	11
Philadelphia	78	71	.523	12½
Cincinnati	73	73	.517	13½
Chicago	75	73	.507	13
Pittsburgh	70	77	.476	19½
Houston	55	93	.372	35
New York	49	99	.331	41

Friday's Results

Chicago 3, Cincinnati 2
Houston 1, New York 0
St. Louis 7, Milwaukee 0
Pittsburgh 5, San Francisco 1 (13 innings)
Philadelphia 3-1, Los Angeles 2-1

Today's Games

Los Angeles at Philadelphia
San Francisco at Pittsburgh
Cincinnati at Chicago
Houston at New York
Milwaukee at St. Louis

Sundays Games

Houston at New York (2)
Los Angeles at Philadelphia
San Francisco at Pittsburgh
Cincinnati at Chicago
Milwaukee at St. Louis (2)

American League

	W.	L.	Pct.	G.B.
x New York	96	51	.658	—
Minnesota	84	65	.564	14
Chicago	84	65	.564	15

The CASE has now been made. It is time for the State of Michigan, and its athletic association, to correct a 61-year error. On September 13, 1963, Loretto won the game vs. St. Ignace with 33-13.

So, here's a special note to the State of Michigan, and its Department of the Athletic Association that deals with game statistics. The CASE has been made, please read it. It's time to turn back the clock and correct a simple grammar error that's lasted for 61 years. The football game, held between St. Ignace and Sault Loretto on September 13, 1963, was won by the Sault Loretto Angels team with a score of 33-13, and not 13-13 as records indicate. Please correct it! Special thanks to Peter Campbell for his digging and fighting. For the truth, BYREE would be proud of us all.

So, here's to you, Paul! You were right. But your fight for the truth has not ended. We, your friends, must get it changed, and hopefully this book will help. As you said, "It's not over till that fat lady sings." She hasn't sung yet. RIP, dear friend. We got this one!

BYREE, Paul Byron, 50th Reunion of Loretto Catholic, 2016. RIP, dear friend.

CHAPTER 7

The Founding of Payment on Sugar Island

My mother's mother, our grandmother Trempe's maiden name, was Mary Payment. Growing up as a young girl, everyone called her Maude. We heard so many stories of her father, Grampa Felix Payment, who was born on Payment in Sugar Island. She said, "He loved building things, and he built the two homes on Cedar Street, one for Gram and her family, and the other for his son, Uncle Chubb and his family. When he spoke, it was in broken English, as his first language was French. What we didn't know much about was the little hamlet on Sugar Island called Payment's Landing, and just how it came to be. As I said, he was born there, in the very place founded by his Payment family. We knew there were plenty of intermarriages there with the local native population and the Indian Reserve at Garden River. It was a major trading post with Sugar Island, and its hamlet of Payment, founded by Felix's uncle, Michael Payment. The two regions of the St. Mary's River were closely linked in time, never mind a border. It was just 100 yards away, which is why it took so long for the British and U.S. governments to settle the boundary issues and disputes. They were finally settled in the 1840s.

Growing up in the Soo, there seemed to be Payments everywhere. In school, in sports, in church, even at the Red Owl store shopping market, they were everywhere—and Mother would say softly, "They are your cousins." What we know is that Grampa Payment, who retired at the Soo Locks and lived till he was 88, came from a family of builders and carpenters. What brought them from the shores of Pointe-Claire, Quebec just outside of Montreal, was they were excellent boat builders.

They were early settlers to a remote fishing village 12 miles northeast of Sault Ste. Marie. They named it Payment on Sugar Island, Michigan. It was barely a hundred yards from Garden River Reserve in Canada and a short ferry boat ride across the St. Mary's River. A British and American dispute over the island's ownership lasted sixty years until 1842 when a treaty placed Sugar Island in American hands. It had been called St. George's Island by the British, and Maple Sugar Island by the Native Chippewas for its abundant maple trees.

It all seemed to begin with the father of all the Payments in Canada. Francois Payment, whose grandparents came to Montreal, Canada from Brittany, France in the 1730s, set up a business to assist the fur traders that were booming throughout the Great Lakes region and the North and building their boats and canoes. They were all skilled craftsmen and knew their trade well. Mr. Francois Xavier Payment was born on March 20, 1781, in Ste. Genevieve in Quebec, Canada. He died on December 13, 1843, in Rigaud, Quebec. He married Josette Fortier on July 30, 1804, in Ste. Joachim, Ontario, Canada. She was the daughter of Jacques Fortier and Amable Leroux. She moved with her sons shortly after the death of her husband, to Payment, Michigan, and died on August 15, 1873, in Garden River, Ontario, Canada.

FRANCOIS PAYMENT and JOSETTE FORTIER had ten children, and it was the members of this family, beginning with Michael G. who trained in Detroit in the Mercantile business and set up a trading post working in the markets of Detroit, Mackinac, and Sugar Island. This brought the family to Garden River. They made the trip up North and crossed over to the East channel and found the hamlet of Payment. There they set up their businesses and flourished for a short while as boat builders, which was the main means of transport at the time, with horses on the narrow paths.

Here are their children:

i.   FRANCOIS XAVIER6 PAYMENT, b. 17 Jan 1810, Pte. Claire, Quebec, Canada.

ii. JOSEPH PAYMENT, b. 07 Apr 1806; d. 11 Aug 1891, Sugar Island, Michigan.

iii. JOSEPHTE PAYMENT, b. 08 May 1807.

iv. EMELIE PAYMENT, b. 25 Sep 1811.

v.   FELICITE PAYMENT, b. 30 Nov 1815; d. 21 Jan 1893, Garden River, Ontario/Canada.

Felicite never got married. Instead, she devoted her life to the ' JESUIT PRIEST' at Garden River, Ontario, Canada.

In her days, when you took on the job as a housekeeper in the Priest's home, you were not allowed to be married. They took a vow of chastity.

Today, married couples take turns with getting the Altar ready for Mass and whatever else has to be done.

vi. MICHAEL GEOFFREY PAYMENT, b. 21 June 1814, Pointe-Claire, Canada; d. 18 Apr 1891, Bay City, Michigan. He is one of the founders, with a vested interest in establishing his trading post. He became known as "The King of Sugar Island."

vii. VERONIQUE ROSE PAYMENT, b. Abt. 1817; d. 10 Feb 1888, Bay City, Michigan.

Notes for VERONIQUE ROSE PAYMENT:

The announcement in last evening's press of the death of Miss Rose Payment was received with the utmost sadness by a large circle of friends, as well as her relatives. Miss Payment was 71 years of age, went to Sugar Island ten miles from Soo, 38 years ago, to her brother. She has since been a mother to his children, caring for them as tenderly as if they had been her own. She moved with her brother to Detroit eighteen years ago, and then to Bay City. She has always been a consistent Christian lady and notable in all works of charity, being a special friend to the poor and distressed, who will sadly miss her kindly and gentle way. Her remains will be taken to Sugar Island for interment beside her mother, brother, and uncle.

viii. FELIX MOISE PAYMENT, b. 20 July 1819; d. 26 July 1882, Sault Ste. Marie, Michigan. This would be Mary Payment's Grandparents, our Felix Payment's Father.

ix. PIERRE ALFRED PAYMENT, b. 26 July 1820.

x. MARGUERITE PAYMENT, b. 28 Nov 1835; d. 01 Feb 1916, Barron, Wisconsin; m. JOSEPH RICHARDS, 15 Apr 1859.

As I stated earlier, it was the Treaty of 1840 and the Jay Treaty of 1794, that brought the Payment family from Pointe-Claire Quebec across the east channel of the river from Garden River, Ontario, Canada. They built the first log house and started a trading post. Later the Payments were followed by the Brassar, Church, Corbiere, Mastaw, McFarlane, McKerchie, McCoy and LeCoy, Menard, Myott, Sayer, and Sebastian families. A fishing village developed along the east channel of the river across from Canada. The Sugar Island Post Office was established on January 13, 1857, with Michael G. Payment as its first postmaster. That year, the village's Holy Angels Church was built, and just down the road the first little log schoolhouse. Bishop Baraga is said to have performed several baptisms in the church in 1862.

Holy Angels Church with land donated by Bishop Baraga, built by Michael Payment.

Philetus S. Church House built a sawmill, store, and a dock called Church's Landing from where his maple syrup and raspberry jam were shipped. He succeeded Michael G. Payment as postmaster on June 8, 1858.

The Sugar Island Post Office discontinued operation on November 9, 1861. Mr. Church was also the township supervisor.

Payment never prospered as a lumber town in its early days. The entire 21-mile-long island had barely more than 200 residents before 1870. Canoeing and horseback were the only means of transport. The island never had a railroad, and there was no ferry service of any kind from the mainland for the first 40 years. The first crude rafts to get people and supplies across the river came with the missionaries in the 1880s, and this led to Payment's brief period of progress.

By 1890 the population had tripled, and the village had several stores, a larger schoolhouse, and several commercial fishing operations. After 1915, the long rough ride on a rutted dirt road from the dock began to decline. The few cars that got across the river were often stuck on the island in the mud. Little by little, other sections of the island were developed, especially after 1925 when regular Sugar Island Ferry service began.

The island and the village began to enjoy better days again. Virtually everything else from Payment's early days is gone. The post office closed in 1942. There is only the church, which is starting to deteriorate. The rest of the island, now with more than 600 year-round residents, has two stores, a restaurant and bar and a community center.

The Payment, MI Post Office (Sugar Island Township) was established on December 19, 1892, with James S. Shields as its first Postmaster.

Payment, MI last day of use postmark dated September 30, 1942

POSTMASTERS THAT HAVE SERVED AT THE PAYMENT, MI POST OFFICE

James S. Shields. . . . . .December 19, 1892

Angus McCoy. . . . . .February 10, 1904

George Adams. . . . . October 29, 1937

Mrs. Veronica E. Edwards. . . . . . December 22, 1938

Angus McCoy. . . . . October 6, 1941 to September 30, 1942

The last day of operation; with mail service to Baie de Wasai.

FELIX PAYMENT married CATHERINE THIBAULT in Pointe-Claire, Quebec. These were my grandmother's grandparents, and my mother's great-grandparents . These were their children:

i.   I ALPHONSE7 PAYMENT, b. 25 Mar 1855, Sugar Island, Michigan; d. 25 Apr 1931, Sault Ste, Marie, Michigan.

ii. MARIE ERMINE EMELIE PAYMENT, b. 08 Jun 1856.

iii. FELIX PAYMENT, b. 13 June 1858, Sugar Island, Michigan; d. 11 Feb 1946, Sault Ste, Marie, Michigan. This is my grandmother's father. My mother's grandfather. The fellow we all called Grampa Payment.

iv. LOUIS JOSEPH PAYMENT, b. 20 Apr 1860, Payment, Sugar Island, Michigan.

v.   ADELAID PAYMENT, b. 19 Jan 1866.

vi. ANGELIQUE PAYMENT, b. 14 Feb 1868, Payment, Sugar Island, Michigan; d. 25 Nov 1948, Ontario, Canada.

vii. ANDREW PAYMENT. Andrew was 28 years of age when he died of a gunshot wound

Gramma's Father and Mother: FELIX PAYMENT (FELIX MOISE) was born on 13 June 1858 in Sugar Island, Michigan, and died on 11 Feb 1946 in Sault Ste, Marie, Michigan. He married (1) MARGUERITE to SYLVESTER, daughter of LOUIS SYLVESTER and LOIS LEVENS. Louis

Sylvester, himself and his family for generations, was an Ontario Métis, and Lois' parents came from England. She was one of the very early settlers in Garden River. Marguerite was born 15 Oct 1861, and she died 18 Oct 1891. Marguerite was recognized as a Jay Treaty Indian, as the Sylvester family signed the Indian Roll in the early 1800s . As a citizen of both Countries, she could travel freely and was a citizen of North America. She had two children, her son Clement was born in 1887. He was our Uncle Chubb, and he looked every bit like a Métis or Native to Canada and America. Her daughter, Mary, was born in December 1889. She was our grandmother, and she too was a designated Métis. Which is how she was accepted by the Ursuline Sisters at their Convent and School. For purposes of introduction, the word Métis is well known in Canada as one of the indigenous peoples of Canada. The name was formerly used in the Sault in the mid to late 1800 s then derogatory terms were used to describe them as "half-breeds" and conquered people. The race of Chippewa, Ottawa, or Algonquin Indians mixed with European lineage are Métis, and they live among us in the Sault today. We have thousands of them in the Sault, and it includes most of the Payment clan. They deserve to be treated kindly, and respected as human beings, not disregarded. It's simply who we are. We are Indigenous people here in America.

Felix Payment, 88, a retired lockman, died at his home, 810 Cedar Street, at 7:35 a.m. today. February 11, 1946, after an illness of four days. Born on Sugar Island, on June 13, 1858, Mr. Payment began work on the locks in 1880, retiring on November 30, 1927.

Great-grandfather Felix Moses Payment

I wish they were all alive today, as now their family history has been identified and preserved once again. I know my mother would be extremely happy and Gramma so very proud. You see, her mother, from Garden River, was Margarite (Rose) Sylvester and died when Gramma was just two years old. Felix, her father, used to bring her over to meet the family left in Payment when she was home from school in St. Ignace.

Because she was a Native American and Métis, Felix had arranged with the sisters at the Ursuline Convent to raise and care for his daughter. She had a wonderful education, and her surrogate mother was a lovely nun who raised her, a Mother St. Francis. Felix, her dad, wanted Gram to be raised as a French lady with a proper Catholic education. And he, certainly, got what he wanted. She was an amazingly devoted mother, a strong woman who was very well-educated in the early 1900s, and a loving grandmother. She named my mother, her seventh child, in honor of Mother St. Francis, and mom kept her picture on her dresser all of her life.

PICTURES OF POINTE-CLAIRE, QUEBEC TODAY

Story above contributed by Paul Petosky— Taken from " Michigan Shadow Towns"

A study of vanishing and vibrant villages by Gene Scott.

Thanks also to Ancestry.com. and Wikipedia.

CHAPTER 8

French Songs From Mom And Gramma

My Mother and grandmother Trempe were great at making certain the McCarthy children knew they were a part of French ancestry too. In other words, we all knew we were Irish, but we were also French through my mother's family. The Trempe's were a prominent French family, coming here from Quebec to the Sault in the 1840 s-1850 s . My grandfather's grandfather, the first settler of our Trempe family coming to the Sault, was Joseph Alfred Piet Trempe. He was born on 05 May 1833 and came to Sault Ste Marie from St. Ambroise de Kildaire, Quebec, Canada in the early 1850s . He and his wife, Rose Anne Dolar, settled in the Grand Trempe Boulevard section of the Sault's West End. His first cousin was Louis P. Trempe, the Postmaster of the Sault, and a very important business merchant and community leader with several business interests. He also was a local philanthropist, and he helped financially with the construction of the Cathedral of St. Mary's Church. Louis convinced his cousin Joseph, the Sault was a booming town, and opportunities were abundant. It is a place for a young man and his family. Grampa's father was Joseph Trempe born in 1856, here in the Sault. He worked in the

Trempe family businesses. He died relatively young, when Grampa was just a teenager. My grandfather's name was Henry Piet Trempe. He was a tradesman and a machine toolmaker. He worked at Soo Machine and Tool Company in Sault Ontario until he retired. He then moved back to Sault Michigan where he was born, after raising his family in Canada for 35 years. Gramma, as I mention later in the book, was educated and raised by the Ursuline Sisters in St. Ignace. Her father, Felix Payment, wanted his daughter to be raised as a proper French lady with a bilingual education. By the time she left school and married Grandpa at 16, she was quite the woman.

My Grandfather, Henry Piet Trempe

So, between her and Mom we were drilled and drilled with French words, numbers, sayings, and songs. But it was fun learning words like Bonjour for good morning, Bonne Nuit for good night, Aujourd hui for today, and Tres Bien for very good. Merci beaucoup for thank you very much, or just Merci for thanks, Je t'en Prie for You're welcome. Comment Allez-Vous for how are you, and Gramma's favorite was Ferme votre grande bouche, which means 'shut your big fat mouth.' But if you wanted to get really fancy, you could say to Gramma in the morning, ' Bon Jour grand-mere,' and comment 'Allez-vous aujourd'hui?' In other words, ' Good morning, Gramma. How are you today?' Then it was our turn to say the numbers 1-10, so we began, un, deux, trois, quatre, cinq, six, sept, huit, neuf, and dix. It didn't take us long really before we all got it, but then came phrases and that was a bit too much at times. It would start something like this, Bonjour Michel, comment allez-vous . When the fun ended and the real testing occurred, I would answer in English and say, "I'm good, Gramma. How are you?"

The songs they left us with were nice children's songs, and many people we grew up with knew them. The first was our famous 'Brother John' song. I used to tease my brother John as this was about him. It went like this; it was very simple but very cute.

FRERE JACQUES

French Lyrics

Frère Jacques

Frère Jacques

Dormez vous?

Dormez vous?

Sonnez les matines

Sonnez les matines

Ding ding dong

Ding ding dong

English

Are you sleeping?

Are you sleeping?

Brother John

Brother John?

Morning bells are ringing

Morning bells are ringing

Ding ding dong

Ding ding dong

I had to ask, 'Was Frère Jacques about a lazy monk?' According to tradition, it is thought the French nursery rhyme, 'Frère Jacques',' is about a friar who has overslept and forgotten to ring the bells for the matins (a service of the Christian Church). It is thought to date to around 1780.

The next up after singing Frere Jacques a hundred times or more was the famous Alouette Song.

Alouette Song

Talking of cruelty, I thought, how about a song about butchery? Alouettes, or larks, have their feathers plucked in this song. First the head, then the beak (odd, beaks aren't feathered), and then the neck and back. The breast of the bird, where most meat and feathers are found, isn't plucked.

Alouette, gentille alouette

Alouette, je te plumerai

Je te plumerai la tête

Je te plumerai la tête

Et la tête, et la tête

Alouette, Alouette

Oh, oh, oh, oh

Alouette, gentille alouette

Alouette, je te plumerai

Je te plumerai le bec

Je te plumerai le bec

Et le bec, et le bec

Et la tête, et la tête

Alouette, Alouette

Oh, oh, oh, oh

Alouette, gentille alouette

Alouette, je te plumerai

Je te plumerai le cou

Je te plumerai le cou

Et le cou, et le cou

Et le bec, et le bec

Et la tête, et la tête

Alouette, Alouette

Oh, oh, oh, oh

Alouette, gentille alouette

Alouette, je te plumerai

Je te plumerai les ailes

Je te plumerai les ailes

Et les ailes, et les ailes

Et le cou, et le cou

Et le bec, et le bec

Et la tête, et la tête

Alouette, Alouette

Oh, oh, oh, oh

Alouette, gentille alouette

Alouette, je te plumerai

Je te plumerai le dos

Je te plumerai le dos

Et le dos, et le dos

Et les ailes, et les ailes

Et le cou, et le cou

Et le bec, et le bec

Et la tête, et la tête

Alouette, Alouette

Oh, oh, oh, oh

Alouette, gentille alouette

Alouette, je te plumerai

Je te plumerai les pattes

Je te plumerai les pattes

Et les pattes, et les pattes

Et le dos, et le dos

Et les ailes, et les ailes

Et le cou, et le cou

Et le bec, et le bec

Et la tête, et la tête

Alouette, Alouette

Oh, oh, oh, oh

Alouette, gentille alouette

Alouette, je te plumerai

Je te plumerai la queue

Je te plumerai la queue

Et la queue, et la queue

Et les pattes, et les pattes

Et le dos, et le dos

Et les ailes, et les ailes

Et le cou, et le cou

Et le bec, et le bec

Et la tête, et la tête

Alouette, Alouette

Oh, oh, oh, oh, oh

It was always fun singing this song as Gramma would tell us and show us what to do. And we laughed and really enjoyed it. After she passed, we tried singing it ourselves and Mom would help us, but it wasn't the same. Every time I hear the song today, I picture my grandmother acting out the Alouette Song. God loves her.

Alouette" (pronounced [alwɛt]) is a popular Quebecois children's song, commonly thought to be about plucking the feathers from a lark.

While the origin remains unclear, some believe it originated in France. The first known French publication of the song came 14 years after the 1879 work from McGill University in Montréal.

The last of the songs I remember that both mom and Gramma sang was about a little boat, called a Little Ship.

There Was a Little Ship

Children's Song

French Lyrics With English Translation

1 Il était un petit navire (bis) Qui n'avait ja-ja-jamais navigué (bis).	1 There was (once) a little ship (twice) That had never sailed (before). (twice)

| 2 Il partit pour un long voyage Sur la mer Mé-Mé-Méditerranée. | 2 It left for a long voyage On the Mediterranean Sea. |
| 3 Au bout de cinq à six semaines, Les vivres vin-vin-vinrent à manquer. | 3 At the end of five or six weeks |

Gramma Trempe, our French teacher, Mary (Maude) Payment Trempe

That was the sum of our French at home. In high school, I studied French for two years. So, we enjoyed it and to be honest, years later as I traveled to France on business, it just took me a few days before things came back to me in conversation. But, speaking at a business luncheon outside of Paris, and upon being introduced, of course, I had to mention my French grandmother, with her favorite French saying. "Michel, Fermez votre grande bouche." It always received a good laugh . You gals did a good job— Mom and Gramma.

CHAPTER 9

Pop's Lumberjack Songs

Our grandfather, on my father's side, was called Pop. His given name was also John T. McCarthy, the very same as my father's and his father's name. For eight generations, the name has been passed down. My great nephew today, John T. wears the name today with pride. Pop lived with us for the last five years of his life. He meant everything to each one of my family. He had all kinds of stories and songs too, and we enjoyed each one of them.

Pop first came to the Upper Peninsula in 1897 from Alliston, Ontario, a small town of Irish, Scottish, and English immigrants outside of Toronto, near the town of Goderich, Ontario. He and his eight brothers and sisters and their parents, John T and Susannah Cox McCarthy, sailed to Sault Ste Marie and landed as indentured servants to John A MacDonald, a prominent Scot, and a large builder in Chippewa County. The population of the Sault was significantly growing back then, a home-building boom was occurring, and new immigrants were all moving to what was considered a fast-growing town, with land to homestead and opportunities everywhere. The family were given shelter on Magazine Street in the Sault and began their service. Their bond was for three years, but everyone chipped in and worked to pay Mr.

MacDonald's passage, and in two years the debt had been paid. The family immediately purchased a horse and wagon and went down the Mackinac trail, homesteaded on their 160 acres, and built their home in the small hamlet of Tone, living near other Irish immigrants, just 5 miles north of Pickford.

Pickford was founded in the 1870s by an Englishman by the name of Charles Pickford. Soon after, a number of Scot Presbyterians. From Goderich, Ontario, they built homes there as well. My grandfather, being the oldest son, immediately vowed with his father and brothers, Mike and Bill, to never work for another man again. They started their own portable sawmill and shingle mill. Although it was portable, and they moved around the County where leases for timber could be arranged, the Rockview Cut between Donaldson and Pickford was their main location. Lumber, fishing, and agriculture were the Kings of the County economy at the time, and they had some good years but also some lean ones. It was in 1910 when a fatal accident took up the life of Pop's father, John T McCarthy. A timber slab shot backwards going through its first cut at the mill, and shot right through his stomach like a bullet, and killed him almost instantly. It was a hard blow, losing his father. For the next five years, Pop took off for the lumber camps in Seney and Grand Marais, as he couldn't face and accept his father's death. They were extremely close, and Pop was the bachelor, and the oldest son still living at home. It was a common practice in many immigrant families, maybe unusual today, but then it was well practiced. So, for the next five years, Pop worked at Seney then took the railroad to Grand Marais as there were no roads at that time, just the rail. The Seney's mills were shutting down, and just a few remained of the 15 large mills they once had. The next big cut was in Grand Marais, on the shores of Lake Superior. He came home in early 1915, for the funeral of his mother. While home, the family had arranged an engagement and marriage to Julia Hassett, my grandmother, whom we fondly called Ma.

On August 1, 1916, Pop and Ma were married. They were married for 37 years when Ma passed away in 1953. Pop was a collector of stories and songs himself, from his time in the lumber camps. He enjoyed and really loved telling his stories to all the old men he gathered with, but with his grandkids, I always felt he was the happiest telling us. He had some favorite songs that he picked up in the lumber camps that were popular at that time in the early 1900s . He would whistle them and hum them, but he truly enjoyed singing them. I think there were at least three songs that I remember well that he always sang. And his stories and tales were endless. But the first song was a Civil War song about a young Irish man coming home after the war. A song against the tragedy of war. It was popular in sawmills at that time.

Johnny, I Hardly Knew Ye was the name of the tune. His very special and favorite verse was:

> *You haven't an arm and you haven't a leg,*
>
> *Hurroo! hurroo!*
>
> *You haven't an arm and you haven't a leg,*
>
> *Hurroo! hurroo!*
>
> *You haven't an arm and you haven't a leg,*
>
> *You're an eyeless, noseless, chickenless egg;*
>
> *You'll have to be put with a bowl to beg:*

He had a deep fondness for the old song ,' a tragic love ballad originally from Scotland. It was one of his favorites, and he enjoyed it immensely.

And slowly she went to him,

And the only words to him did say

Was, Young man, I think you're dying.

He turned his face unto the wall

And turned his back upon her,

"Goodbye, goodbye to all my friends,

But be kind, be kind to Barbara Allen.

There are several other verses, but his voice always trembled it seemed like when he finished the song.

They buried Willie in the old churchyard

And Sweet Barbara in the new one

And on William's grave, there grew a rose

And Barbara Allen's, a green briar.

They grew and grew in the old churchyard

Till they could grow no higher

And there they tied in a true lover's knot

The red rose grew 'round the briar.

The older I get, the more I appreciate Pop. He was quite the man. He was just a lumberjack, a skilled sawyer, he liked to be called. Likewise, he would say, he just got to the second book with his education. So, he urged us to study hard. I remember so well, he had the most difficult time writing his name. But he refused to sign it with an X. He was a man to be honored, respected, and regarded. We loved him.

The last song he always sang to all his grandkids was 'Buffalo Gals.' They sang it in the lumber mills and camps. When they were cutting, a logger would always start the song and everyone chipped in. He wanted each of us to sing it with him.

My grandfather, Pop, John T McCarthy, Logger, Sawyer.

Buffalo Gals

Buffalo Gals, won't you come out tonight,

Come out tonight, come out tonight.

Buffalo Gals, won't you come out tonight

And dance by the light of the moon.

As I was walking down the street,

Down the street, down the street,

A pretty little gal I chanced to meet,

Oh, she was fair to see.

Buffalo Gals, won't you come out tonight,

Come out tonight, come out tonight.

Buffalo Gals, won't you come out tonight

And dance by the light of the moon.

I stopped her and we had a talk,

Had a talk, had a talk,

Her feet took up the whole sidewalk

And left no room for me.

Buffalo Gals, won't you come out tonight,

Come out tonight, come out tonight.

Buffalo Gals, won't you come out tonight

And dance by the light of the moon.

I asked her if she'd have a dance,

Have a dance, have a dance,

I thought that I might have a chance

To shake a foot with her.

Buffalo Gals, won't you come out tonight,

Come out tonight, come out tonight.

Buffalo Gals, won't you come out tonight

And dance by the light of the moon.

I danced with a gal with a hole in her stockin',

And her heel kept a-knockin', and her toes kept a-rockin'

I danced with a gal with a hole in her stockin'

And we danced by the light of the moon.

Buffalo Gals, won't you come out tonight,

Come out tonight, come out tonight.

Buffalo Gals, won't you come out tonight?

And dance by the light of the moon.

A little history of the Irish and the Civil War songs that were popular at that time. The Civil War had a great impact on the Irish immigrant and his family. Over 600,00 Irish signed up and served in the Union side with their families promised immediate citizenship, and another 140,000 signed up and fought for the Confederacy with also a promise of citizenship if they won. Isn't it an interesting part of our history? Shortly after the Civil War until the early 1910s, with the human commitment to our Country's Republic, the Irish were to be hit with, "Irish No Need to Apply," as they sought work and basic survival. One must ask, are we really repeating our history today?

Photo taken in Grand Marais

Seney Lumber Camps

CHAPTER 10

Mom Singing Auld Lang Syne

My mother (God bless her!) sang every New Year's Eve the Scots ballad, Auld Lang Syne. It was traditional in Canada, and it was how she was raised in Soo, Ontario. Her Scottish Canadian neighbors and the Scottish friends of her parents taught her the song. And as she would tell my father when he sings it during the New Year's festivities, "No, Jack, it's sung this way."

And with her learned Highland Scot dialect, she would sing the song. Now, she also had to interpret for us the Scottish words and phrases in the song. It wasn't English as we knew it. But a beautiful separate dialect and distinct language of Scots Gaelic. One should not forget one's old friends, which is the basis of the song. The version of the song we sing today is based on a poem published by Robert Burns, which he attributed to "an old man's singing," noting that it was a traditional Scottish song. Everyone likes a good party, and the end of one year and the beginning of the next seems like as good a thing to celebrate as anything else, so Scottish-inflected New Year's celebrations with its Calvinist and Presbyterian leanings— including the sentimental and appealingly nonspecific "Auld Lang Syne"—came naturally to the English-speaking world.

Every New Year, we gathered around the radio, and later the television, to watch Guy Lombardo make "Auld Lang Syne" a tradition. From 1929 to 1976, Lombardo and his Royal Canadians captivated audiences, including our part of the UP, with their annual New Year's Eve broadcasts. Lombardo, a Canadian bandleader whose parents were Italian immigrants, became a cultural staple, with Americans tuning in year after year to celebrate the occasion with his big band music.

It was a wonderful way to say goodbye, offer good luck, or truly wish for happiness ahead. My mother, with all of us, held a special place during this moment, as she carried the knowledge and history of the song—not my dad. She would softly, and with meaning, recite the song's lyrics and reflect on how we best remember the memories of the past, our friends we love, and the experiences we all shared.

So, let's share a cup of kindness as we journey into the New Year.

The original Scots Gaelic words carry a unique beauty, inviting us to follow along and enjoy both the poem and the song.

Auld Lang Syne

The Burns version of the Morgan manuscript

Should auld acquaintance be forgot,

And never brought to mind?

Should auld acquaintance be forgot,

And days o' lang syne!

For auld lang syne, my Dear,

For auld lang syne,

We 'll tak a cup o ' kindness yet,

For auld lang syne.

We twa hae run about the braes,

And pu 't the gowans fine;

But we 've wander 'd mony a weary foot,

Sin auld lang syne.

We twa hae paidlet i ' the burn,

Frae mornin ' sun till dine:

But seas between us braid hae roar 'd,

Sin auld lang syne.

And there 's a hand, my trusty feire,

And gie 's a hand o ' thine;

And we 'll tak a right gude-willie waught,

For auld lang syne.

And surely ye 'll be your pint-stowp,

And surely I'll be mine;

And we'll tak a cup o' kindness yet, For auld lang syne.

My dear mother, Frances Martha McCarthy

In Irish Gaelic, allow this Canadian Yooper to say—Go mbeirimíd beo ar an am seo arís. Go Raibh Maith Agat. (That we all may gather again this time next year). Thank you!

CHAPTER 11

The French Hamlet Of Keldon

Growing up, I heard of the stories of how the early settlers named the village they helped to settle, with their name. So why not name your town or village to glorify your name ? I thought and used to question my dad all the time, "Why did they do that"? The Sault was named in honor of the Rapids and St. Mary, and St. Ignace in honor of St. Ignatius, both of those made sense. But look at the other names of towns and villages of the EUP. We had Pickford, Rudyard, Payment, Newberry, Curtis, Stirlingville, McCarron, Ransonville, Barbeau, and Donaldson; all were named for their founders and early settlers. I'm sure there are others too. But then we had our ghost towns in the county as well. The few I remember best were Shelldrake, MI, named after the company who owned the town. Once with 1,000 people living there, now it is just a few old buildings. Another was Seewhy, MI, in Chippewa County's Hulbert Township, which was the odd-named ghost town of Seewhy. The small town was named after C.Y. Bennett, who took it upon himself to name the town after himself. C.Y. already had his own sawmill and general store.

Then we had Fibre, MI. I remember this one the best as there used to be some good streams and beaver dams near there, and we used Fibre as the location to hike in. Although, it was a few miles from there. The Michigan Ghost Town of Fibre, in Chippewa County, is one of those lost Michigan towns that still legally exist, but you would never know it if you drove through it. All that remains is an old store and railroad— and that's about it. What we know about Fibre—and there is little—is that it began life as a railroad station in 1891 along the Minnesota, St. Paul & Sault Ste. Marie Railway. A post office opened on July 10, 1895, under the name 'Alberta' and changed the name to 'Fibre' on January 20, 1896. The post office lasted for years until it closed for good on June 10, 1985. Fibre can be found in Chippewa County's Rudyard Township at the railroad crossing over Trout Lake Road.

But there is one special little hamlet in Pickford Township that has kept its post office for years. The settlement itself has its descendants of the original families who settled there, and that little dear village is called KELDON. It was always a favorite of mine as the names of its early settlers began with Donah Desormeaux in 1855, then came more Desormeaux's, Fortins', LaJoie's, Benoit's, Libby's, Potvin's, Coullard's, Carriere's, Castagne's, and Bourgond's. These were the same names of the grandkids I went to school with. It was a colorful region of the county, filled with great storytellers, and people who loved to fish, and especially hunt. The stories they would weave could keep you up all night laughing. Also, My Dad used to take us there and fish in the Desormeaux Creek, a great little trout stream that flowed through parts of Keldon right to the Munuscong River. We always caught some fish, and then he would stop by a friend he knew in Keldon and enjoy a few drinks.

In the early 1900s, one of the leading industrial families of Michigan was the Dodge Brothers, Horace, and John Dodge. The Dodge Motor Company at that time through 1920, when both brothers passed away, was the fourth largest car manufacturer in the United States. During the early years of 1900 and the first years of prohibition, the brothers enjoyed Keldon. They purchased 500 hundred acres in the Keldon area near the Munuscong River leading to the Bay, and a significant cabin or lodge was built. They certainly enjoyed fishing and hunting, specifically duck hunting and deer hunting. Furthermore, they were great friends to the local population, and it was a practice of the brothers to have celebrations with the locals to honor their citizens. They gave their large parcel of land to the State of Michigan, and Dodge Park today is a part of the 14,000-acre Munuscong Bay State Park.

Dodge Brothers Lodge (started the Dodge Car Co. in Detroit) on Munuscong Lake. Called Munuscong Hunting and Fishing Club. Horace Elgin Dodge on left, Fred Postal center John Francis Dodge on right. With deer 1905. They owned approx 500 acres on South side of Munuscong River in Pickford Twp in U. P. of MI

Chippewa County Historical Society

It was the Homestead Act of 1862 that brought a flood of immigrants up to the EUP. It was during the 1880s-1900s that the agricultural output from the County was very high. The new settlers cleared the land and farmed it. Chippewa County had become a leading agricultural region in the state, while the lumber boom was still going strong. The population was booming, and the Sault was destined to be the next Chicago.

The founder and Keldon's early settlers came from The Province of Quebec in Canada. They spoke French as their first language, but then as they learned to speak English, they began speaking a form of broken French, much like the families of Payment on Sugar Island. They had their own elementary school for a number of years that eventually closed. The students then walked 4–5 miles into Pickford for their official education. In 1890, they had their own post office and remained open for years. Today they are serviced from the post office in Pickford.

My Irish grandparents had several friends who lived in Keldon and a few of the men would work at the McCarthy Mill. The two communities of Tone being Irish Catholic and Keldon being French Catholic invited one another to parties, dances, weddings, and picnics. One of the great stories Dad would tell, chatting with George LaJoie, was about his father and mother going to a celebration dance in the French community. This was in the 1920s during Prohibition times. A local resident, Claffis Desormeaux, and my grandmother were great dance partners. They were dancing to a waltz, when Pop would go out into the kitchen with several of the men, and George's Dad was one of them. They each would "take a swig or two" of some special moonshine, and I could just picture the chatter. My Dad would say Pop said it was the best moonshine in the entire County. In fact, our county history has recorded a story of Keldon's wealth. Of course, during prohibition, it originally paved a picture giving an appearance of poverty in the years prior to 1918. Most of the buildings were in disrepair. But once Prohibition passed, sleepy Keldon woke up and became a boom town. Buildings were repaired and painted, and the farming community started to spend their money on new cars and sending their kids to school in Sault Ste Marie. In other words, dramatic economic benefits occurred to the residents of Keldon during Prohibition. The woods around the village had become a forest of illegal stills, and its major source of revenue came from the thirsty populace of Sault Ste Marie.

Those folks and their offspring are some of the finest people in the entire county . We teased each other when we were all young, and they gave as good as they got. But they were true and loyal friends, they were all strong in their citizenship giving back to their community, and strong in their belief in the country . You really must hand it to them—the early settlers of Chippewa County, especially our Quebec settlers. They carved out homes from the forests of the UP, creating solid farms and transforming the land into something fertile. They truly did it right.

CHAPTER 12

The Six Orange Lodges in Chippewa County

Earlier this week, while sorting through old pictures and newspapers, I came across some older editorials from the Sault Evening News. I then came across a picture of the last Orange Parade in Chippewa County, held in Stalwart on July 12, 1957. Really? I thought to myself. I recalled 1957, the year of what I call the Parade of Hate, which highlights why the Orange lodges were formed in the first place. Their deep-rooted disdain for Catholicism and suspicion of Rome's influence in national politics fueled their existence. While the lodges provided a social outlet for members and their families, their foundation lay in celebrating William of Orange's 1690 victory over King James II at the River Boyne, which marked the end of Catholic influence in England and the restoration of civil and religious liberty.

The largest theological differences between Catholic and Protestant Christians are the authority of the Pope and the form of the Eucharist in Communion. Most Protestants broke away from the Catholic Church because they challenged the clergy's and the Pope's authority.

BUT IT'S TIME WE SAT DOWN AND TALKED ABOUT THE ORANGE ORDER.

(A Reddit post from N. Ireland)

I can understand unionism. I can see the points that someone from a unionist background might make to support their opinion, and I respect them. But the Orange Order? They are quite literally the British equivalent of the Klu Klux Klan.

The Orange Order is an ethno-religious sect that believes in the nonsense of its superiority, as demonstrated by the annual 'marching season'. They worship a slave trader. William of Orange wasn't just a trader of slaves, he held the keys to the British Royal African Company, making him responsible for the most profound levels of human misery, with global consequences.

They dress up in distinctive costumes and burn effigies and symbols, often accompanied by messages of hate. Even the pejorative 'Hill Billy' comes from Williamite settlers, who exported their brand of insular hate to the United States. This would not be tolerated in any other modern country. This has no place in the 21st Century. This must be called out for what it is.

In 1795, during a period of Protestant-Catholic sectarian conflict, Ulster Protestants founded the Orange Order in County Armagh as a fraternity sworn to maintain the Protestant Ascendancy in Ireland.

One of Chippewa County's Orange Lodges is located in Sault Ste. Marie, Donaldson, Silverdale, Pickford, Stalwart, and Dafter.

In 1939, six Orange Lodges existed in Chippewa County, located in Sault Ste. Marie, Donaldson, Silverdale, Pickford, Stalwart, and Dafter. At that time, there were a total of 240 Orange Lodges in good standing across the United States. Of those, 15 were active in the state of Michigan, with six right here in Chippewa County. I couldn't believe it when I first learned this, but the stories my dad and my Uncle Donald McDonald (whom we affectionately called "Dongol") told me were indeed true.

Dongol, who was married to my dad's older sister, Doine, grew up in the DeTour Village area of the Upper Peninsula. DeTour was predominantly a Catholic village, where many immigrants had settled. The Sacred Heart

Catholic Church, built there long ago, still stands today. However, surrounding areas such as Raber, Stalwart, and Goetzville were home to several Scottish Presbyterians, and the Orange Lodge became an important meeting place for many of its residents. The lodge's Nativist and Anglican viewpoints played a significant role in shaping those villages.

Growing up, both Dongol and my father, who was raised in Tone, an Irish Catholic hamlet, experienced the deeply rooted animosity between religious groups. This hatred, often linked to the tensions surrounding The Orange Lodge, was a part of their daily lives—whether in school, in sports, or the community.

They grew up the hard way, and they learned very quickly to use their fists to get them through. Orangeism was quite active back then, and it left its scars on these men.

Donald McDonald grew up in DeTour Village. His Father was a lumberman and a Scottish Catholic. Known to his friends as "Dusty", and my family as Dongol, our favorite uncle.

But what were the beliefs of the Orange Lodge? The Order sees itself as defending Protestant civil and religious liberties, while critics accuse it of being sectarian, triumphalist, and supremacist. It did not accept non-Protestants as members unless they converted and adhered to its principles, nor did it accept Protestants married to non-Protestants. The Orange Order had its origins in the 18th century Protestant rural vigilantes, like the 'Peep O'Day Boys', who were set up to fight their Catholic equivalent. Now the craziness of this whole picture can be told better, through our immigration. We received and welcomed openly from Ontario, Canada during the years 1870-1920 many English and Scot-Irish Presbyterians families to Chippewa County. That part was great for our Country, State, and County. It also brought with them, their ancient thinking of a Protestant Ascendancy and Supremacy and that Catholicism was a false belief, comprised of "Statue Worshipers."

In its early years of existence, the Orange Order was one of the most popular civic organizations in Chippewa County. The members enjoyed the fact their culture was a part of a Protestant community. At their annual parades, there were plenty of drummers of all kinds, with flutters and fifes and banners and always a white horse in honor of King Billy himself. There was always playing of the Orange Songs, and among them, you would hear most often was the song called the Orange Flute. It was about a proud Orangemen, a Protestant of course, named Bob who married a Papist, called Bridget. You can let your imagination run free from there. Then there was a tale of our dear family friend Bill Murphy who used to say, "Orangemen's Day is a joke, it's a story of how King William and his 3,000 Dutch fighters beat up 300 Irish Catholics and have been bragging about it ever since." Now, do not pick a fight, as those times are past and gone, and they should remain. But since that last parade of 1957, the Lodges have lost all or most of their membership and all of the lodges have closed. Catholicism after JFK's election has been mainstreamed into American Society, just look at the appointees to the US Supreme Court. Today, we no longer need to see an Orangeman's Day Parade in our county or country. But, here in our Country, they have the right to march if they so choose, and it's protected by our Constitution, under The Right of the Freedom of Speech and The Right to assemble peacefully.

Chippewa County Orange Lodges to Celebrate the Battle of Boyne July 12

Parade and Speaking Program Scheduled at Pickford; William White, Sault, Is General Chairman; Fred Peffers, Marshal

Chippewa county's six Orange lodges will toast King William's victory over James II in the Battle of the Boyne in Ireland in 1690 with the annual celebration at Pickford on July 12.

William White, master of Lodge No. 174 of Sault Ste. Marie, is general chairman of the celebration and Fred Peffers will be grand marshal of the parade.

Speakers will be Thomas McCondra of the Sault, past grand master of Michigan; the Rev. William Combellack of Pickford; Dr. John Ver Straale of the Sault; and Adjutant Bert Curtiss of the Sault.

Parade at 1:30

The parade, characterized by the shrill fifes and robust drumming, will start at 1:30 and the program is scheduled for 2:30, tentatively in the Orange hall at Pickford which will be the headquarters. At 11:30 members of the Ladies Auxiliary of the Presbyterian church of Pickford will serve dinner at the Methodist church parlors.

There are 14 Orange lodges in Michigan, six of them in Chippewa county. The six Orange lodges in the county and their masters are:

174, Sault Ste. Marie, William White.

192, Donaldson, Louis Brownlee.

363, Silverdale, R. Wright.

159, Pickford, Gordon Peffers.

379, Stalwart, Chester Crawford.

152, Dafter, Stewart Hoorastra.

The total number of lodges in good standing in the United States is about 260, Mr. White said.

The Battle of the Boyne which firmly established William, Prince of Orange, on the British throne, was fought nearly 250 years ago.

Left Holland in 1688

William came to England in 1688, only in accordance with the wishes of the mighty, but all sorts and conditions of men, with one accord one mind and one heart, endeavoured to forward it, even the women and children assembled in great congregations in The Netherlands praying to God to bless the Prince of Orange and crown his designs with success."

June Rain New Record for the Soc

Total Last Month 5.86 Heaviest in Fifty Years

Heaviest June rainfall in 50 years was recorded here last month, according to the monthly meteorological summary issued today by Arthur F. Pilppo of the Sault Weather Bureau.

A total of 5.86 inches, the heaviest in weather bureau history which dates back to 1888, was listed in the summary. The rainfall for the month was 2.94 inches above normal mark of 2.92 inches. Only four times since 1889, three times within the last five years, have more than five inches been recorded here.

Temperature for June was normal, or slightly above. The average daily was 55.6 degrees, .2 de

The Orange Flute

In County Tyrone, near the town of Dungannon

Where many a ruction myself had a hand in,

Bob Williamson lived, a weaver by trade,

And all of us thought him a stout Orange blade.

On the 12th of July as around him we'd come,

Bob would play on the flute with a hand on the drum,

You may talk of your harp, your piano and lute,

But they're nothing compared to the old Orange flute.

But Bob, the deceiver, he took us all in,

He married a papish called Bridget McGinn,

Turned papish himself, and forsook the old cause

That gave us all freedom, religion and laws.

...And the fate of the flute now was truly pathetic,

It was fastened and burned at the stake as heretic,

As the flames rose round it they heard a great noise:

'Twas the old flute still playing "The Protestant Boys".

The whole damn ugliness of the Orange Order and Protestant Ascendency was easy to understand. The Protestants considered themselves British, and the Roman Catholics considered themselves Irish. And the problem was they lived in the same country. However, the golden rule was in full effect, and he had the gold rules, which they did and kept for 800 years. That's the way it was, and that's what the people in control had, it was their rules. The unfortunate part of all that was, as they immigrated to come to America, that was not England or Ireland. They couldn't move their power struggles and power base over here. But they sure tried. I have heard great stories over the years from both sides of the issue that some call The Orange and Green.

My wife Judy and I visited Belfast a few years ago, and it was wonderful. Belfast is a beautiful city, and with the Good Friday Peace agreement still intact, the city is working once again without violence. But we did take what was called a ride in the "Black Taxi." The trip took us through the opened doors of the Peace Wall, and we traveled into both sides, where years before there was horrible street violence and killing. It was quite an educational tour. It showed us that deep feelings still persist, and strong emotions are still present. It exists in the neighborhoods divided by the Wall. The commercial sector which drives the economic sector of the community is open and functioning well. For the first time in years, opportunities for Catholics are as strong as ever. Peace is working, and there is a real feeling of renewal in Belfast, and once again it has transformed itself.

One final point, my brothers, John and Tim, and I went over to Ireland in July 1990. We were right there on the River Boyne where the battle took place on July 12th in 1690, three hundred years before. There were some marchers ready to go, and drummers ready to make some noise. My brother Tim often commented after that, he remembers that day as if it happened yesterday. He felt tension and was very uncomfortable just being there. To me, it was a little different, but overall, it was a day in Ireland to be remembered. Up in the north, we saw on RTE that evening of just some small parades—nothing really to speak of. It did make us wonder and think, though, how stupid we humans can be, and we still can be if we are not careful.

The McCarthy Brothers, John, Tim, and Mike, in Ireland July 12, 1990.

CHAPTER 13

Yack (Jack) Kokkinen meet Jack McCarthy

I was just a young boy, probably 7 or 8 years old, when my dad took my brother John and me up into the North Ontario bush. It was my first trip, but John had gone there at least 3 times previously. Dad said to me and Mom, "it's time he comes too, Fran". "Mike, you're coming with me for the weekend to do some fishing". So off we went up the old Highway 17 North to Serchmont, Ontario, just an hour or so out of Sault, Canada. Now that was back in the 1950s, today it's probably just a half hour drive before the turn to Serchmont. But back then, it was a different time and a different road.

The town of Searchmont received its name in honor of T. C. Search, the treasurer of the consolidated Lake Superior Company. Searchmont was once a bustling community built around the forestry industry. The local sawmill was the livelihood of most of the residents. Today it is quite a resort and tourist location.

Serchmont back in the 50s for me, was known for being near Wickstrom Lake and some great trout fishing and Ernie Lee's cabin. It was home to a great ski hill that invited hundreds of skiers during the winter. It was home to my father's lumberjack friend Yack (Jack) Kokkinen. Yack, as he pronounced his Finnish name, was A Canadian lumberjack who worked there in the woods of Searchmont as a logger.

His company had several cutters and a large mill there, but it was the loggers that Yack was part of. He was truly a Legendary character to me, much like Paul Bunyan was to the early loggers in Maine and Minnesota. He was about 6 feet tall and had a very thick chest . His hands were huge, his arms were huge, and his neck was like a tree stump. But he was the greatest, and funniest storyteller I think I have ever heard.

Now to drive to Ernie's cabin and once we got ourselves into Searchmont, we had to drive up an old logging road to the lake. But if you didn't have a jeep or truck, it was impossible to get into without tearing the entire muffler system from your car, if you were silly enough to drive one up that 5 mile trek to the Lake. But once we got there, and hiked into Ernie's cabin, it was like being in heaven, really! It was a spring fed lake, and the fishing was ideal. It was quite a history of Ernie, being an American, finding this property years ago. Being an American, he was limited in terms of ownership, but then he filed for a lease to build on Crown Land, and that's what he did. His original camp, now a beautiful cabin, was the first on this pictorial lake. And we loved going there.

Once we all settled in, on a Saturday, John and I would go fishing. While Dad and Bill Murphy would drive back to Town, and make two stops, the first being, the store, and the next stop and most important stop was the local saloon. Ernie stayed at the cabin with us. It's there, at the saloon, they would run into Yack where he spent most of his time on a Saturday. That is, he did, unless the Mrs. had the same important things she needed to be done . Yack was in his chair at the bar, telling stories, and buying his friends drinks when Dad and Bill walked in.

My Father, John T. McCarthy

Dad and Yack met in the late 1940s, in Searchmont, and became great friends. He emigrated from Finland after WWII, once the Treaty of Paris was signed and finally ended their war with Russia in 1947. He and his young wife came to Canada. He was going to work in the woods of Northern Ontario. He had a very interesting history, I thought. This was the basis of most of his stories. He was a Sergeant in the Finnish Ski Army or Patrol as they were called. The Russo-Finnish war took place in early November 1939 —- March 1940. It was also known as the Winter War. But to Yack, he hated the Russians with a passion, to him, there was nothing worse. He called them Ruskies. "They attacked my Country, and shot me 7 times," he said.

It wasn't long before the boys got Yack out of the saloon and came up to the cabin with Dad and Bill. After a few hours back at Ernie's, the boys kept up their drinking, storytelling, and the laughter was something to talk about. It was loud, very loud, but it was nice as they were surely having fun. Yack talked about one million Russian troops attacking the Fins all along their Country's boundary line. The boundary between Russia and Finland covered over 800 miles and "it was the Ski Patrol that kept the Ruskies at bay and off guard as they couldn't find us or keep up with us." It was Finland's military on skis, and they were sharpshooters and great skiers.

He then would tear off his shirt and show the 7 bullet holes that left their scars in his body. They were real scars for sure where the bullets went through, and it was an unbelievable sight for an 8-year-old boy to see. He would point to each of the scars and named one after each of the Ruskies he had killed during their war.

The men used to talk and ask why Yack chose Canada to come to. What prompted him and his wife to immigrate to Canada. I didn't know this, but apparently it was the US and Canada that gave Finland a bye and supported the country politically and diplomatically after WWII . Finland because of their hatred for Russia was part of the Axis with Germany but didn't really support the German military.

The Finnish army was still fighting Russia with the Germans, in former Finnish land they surrendered initially to Russia. England and France wanted to punish Finland after the war, but Canada and the US stood behind Finland, and said, NO. So, after the final Treaty of Paris in 1947, the War with Russia ended. He and his young wife left for Ontario shortly after, and arrived in Canada in the early months of 1948.

My Dad would take at least three trips a year to Searchmont in all kinds of weather. He loved going to the cabin, loved his friends and wanted to fish and see Yack. The worst trip, and yet the most exciting, for me was when I was 17, a senior in high school. We drove into the lake with our snowmobiles and had to take out the batteries of the snow machines to keep them warm in the cabin, so our machines would start in the morning. The fuel oil pump at the camp had frozen. The men, Yack included, cut down a tree and brought it into the cabin for our heat. That wood stove kept us alive as the temps outside dipped well below zero. Outside, it got as low as 30 degrees below zero. So, we huddled around the stove, and while the men drank their whiskey and beer, I cut up the tree there in the kitchen and fed the stove all night. As cool as it got, the stories and laughter kept it all very light and there was no time to worry, we were all having fun. Yack with his stories of the war in Russia, Dad recounting tales of Australian sailors in New Guinea, Bill sharing memories of standing in picket lines with his father during the copper mine strikes, and Ernie, the first true explorer and settler around Wickstrom Lake, telling of the nonsense he endured because of the Crown Land Fiasco. The point is that he is an American, not a Canadian.

We got off in the morning and the weather was still below zero, but the sun was out. Our warm batteries started our snowmobiles right up. We drove back down the snow trail to our cars, drove Yack home, and then we drove back home to the Sault. Not a word from anyone, as what happens in Searchmont stays in Searchmont. And we didn't even wet a line to do some ice fishing.

These times and stories are never to be forgotten, they were from a different time and different place. But I thank God I lived with them .

CHAPTER 14

Great Stories From The Lumber Camps

I'm certain every kid growing up in the North has heard stories of our legendary hero, Lumberjack Paul Bunyan, and his blue ox Babe. Here's the write-up from Wikipedia: Paul Bunyan is a giant lumberjack and folk hero in American and Canadian folklore. His tall tales revolve around his superhuman labor, and he is customarily accompanied by Babe the Blue Ox, his pet and working animal. The character originated in the oral tradition of North American loggers and was later popularized by freelance writer William B. Laughead (1882–1958) in a 1916 promotional pamphlet for the Red River Lumber Company.

He has been the subject of various literary compositions, musical pieces, commercial works, and theatrical productions. His likeness is displayed in a number of oversized statues across North America.

The tale of his exploits that I enjoyed the most was this one. Bunyan was a powerful giant, seven feet tall and with a stride of seven feet. He was famous throughout the lumbering districts for his great physical strength.

— K. Bernice Stewart & Homer A. Watt, " Legends of Paul Bunyan, Lumberjack"

I thought when I was young and heard this story, I asked my grandfather, Pop, who was a lumberjack too, did he ever know anyone like Paul Bunyan or meet anyone like him. He always smiled when I asked him my 10,000 questions a day, but he did say in Grand Marais and Seney there were a few men, very large in size, good loggers, that could do the work of 5 men. He said to Mikey, "They were strong as a mountain." I didn't know what that really meant back then, but Dad would say, "the logger was very strong".

When they left the logging camp, and moved on to another camp, people talked about them for years. But there are others too who have left their footprint in the Northwoods, and their stories have become legendary. My research has detailed some I can share in this story.

Above George Portice driving a sleigh loaded with logs flattened top and bottom for building the railroad in Pickford. The photo 1900.

Source of White Pine

Figures like Jigger Johnson, the Maine woodsman famous for allegedly kicking knots off frozen logs barefoot, and Joseph Montferrand (better known as Big Joe Mufferaw), the French-Canadian renowned for his strength and dedication to protecting French-speaking loggers, have been celebrated as folk heroes across North America. Their legendary feats have contributed to the enduring myths surrounding the lumberjack.

The man who acquired the worst reputation was P.K. Small; he was given the nickname "Snapjaw" for good reason. Snapjaw lived in the 1880s -1890s in Seney during Michigan's lumber boom; it didn't take long for him to make his reputation as a maniac. This guy either had mental problems or he was raised by bears. And there were others that left a story to tell.

Perhaps the most despicable character to live on in Seney lore is that of Daniel Dunn, whose deadly feud with the Harcourt family made headlines across the nation. The feud began in downstate Roscommon, where Dunn and the Harcourts owned rival saloons.

Dunn had a seamy reputation before coming to Seney in the 1880s, and had served time in a Michigan state prison and in the Detroit House of Corrections. He was a large and powerful man who was known for committing brutal and unprovoked assaults upon anyone who challenged him. Dunn was also suspected of committing at least two unsolved murders while living in Seney.

The Harcourt family, too, had relocated to Seney in the 1880s and had opened a saloon, while Dunn was the proprietor of a "low dive" frequented by prostitutes and toughs. The feud boiled over on June 24, 1891, when a drunken Stephen Harcourt foolishly entered Dunn's establishment and started listing his many crimes. An enraged Dunn shot Harcourt twice before he managed to stagger out of the saloon.

Harcourt died three days later at the home of his mother.

Dunn was brought to Manistique for a preliminary examination before a justice of the peace on murder charges. After only a partial hearing, Dunn was released. It was later learned that he had bribed the county prosecuting attorney, William Riggs, to obtain his freedom. Riggs would later resign in disgrace. But before Dunn left Manistique, he brought charges against John, Richard, and James Harcourt for making threats against his life.

The three Harcourt brothers were arrested one day later in Seney by Sheriff Dennis Heffron and were brought to Trout Lake Junction to await the Soo Line train back to Manistique. Curiously, the Harcourts were not disarmed following their arrest. While waiting for the train, Sheriff Heffron and the three Harcourt brothers entered a saloon near the depot with the intention of buying cigars. Upon entering the saloon, the brothers encountered Dan Dunn standing at the bar. Dunn spotted the Harcourts first and was reaching for his gun when he was killed by five shots from James Harcourt's revolver.

In the aftermath of the shooting, James Harcourt was brought to Sault Ste. Marie to face murder charges in Chippewa County. There, he was convicted and sentenced to spend ten years in the state prison at Marquette, His sentence was commuted by Michigan Governor Rich on May 6, 1895, upon the recommendation of the Board of Pardons. James Harcourt returned to Seney following his release from Marquette. He was later elected as township clerk and served 20 years as the Seney Township Supervisor. James Harcourt died in October 1938 while living in downstate Roscommon.

They were all characters. Some were complete gentlemen, educated men, who came to a logging camp for the money, but they had to learn quickly the life of a logger. While the others were men not of character but a special breed of toughness and individualism. Hardworking man who had a strong back and knew how to wheel an ax and pull a saw. Many too were renegades from the law, rebels from society, and the worst were rogues and scoundrels. We had them all in our camps from Ontonagon County in the western UP to RACO in the eastern UP. Some left their Stories in a poem, like my family.

McCarthy' Sawing Mill

There's wealth in raising cattle,

And there's money made in hay,

The butcher's and the grocer's,

Grow richer everyday.

But there isn't a vocation,

Worked with whatever skill,

Will give its owners pockets,

Like a portable Sawmill.

Between Donaldson and Pickford,

And just about half way,

McCarthy's mill's located,

For a temporary stay.

There from morning till the evening,

You'll find a busy throng,

While the circular and the engine,

Sing a wealth producing song.

At seven every morning,

At the welcome hour of noon,

And at Six each evening,

She whistles up a tune.

Like the howling of some wild beast,

In the distant jungle land,

But it has the Sound of Music,

To her busy hustling band.

Old Johnnie stands with the lever,

In his ever ready hand,

While the mill and me together,

Obey his last command.

John Jr, rides the Carriage,

Sets the timber for the saw,

While Mike attends the engine,

And the boiler's fiery saw.

John Hanna has the cross-cut,

Under his special charge,

And cuts up into stove wood,

All slabs however large.

And John has got the movements,

Intelligence and skill,

To cut more slabs than any man,

That works around the mill.

Hank Johnson's bass rail sawyer,

A lad both strong and quick,

Who very keenly watches,

The slabs are not too thick.

With William draws the timber,

With his doughty well-trained team,

And rolls it on the skid way,

There ends my rhyming theme.

H. Duggan, 1904

The McCarthy Portable Shingle Mill

1910

Grampa McCarthy, head sawyer, Pop, and Uncle Mike.

CHAPTER 15

"My First Buck...
Or Was It My Tenth?"
By Anthony Andary

THE OBSESSION:

You see, oddly enough, my obsession with whitetail deer hunting started when I was four years old. I had attentively listened to my dad (Tony Sr. or Big Tony as most of our family and friends affectionately referred to him) and his deer and duck hunting partner Charlie Madigan, as they would reminisce about deer hunting and tall tales from deer camp since I was a toddler.

I vividly recall that fateful Friday evening in November 1959 when Charlie showed up at our door all dressed in hunter's red, smoking a cigarette, as usual. As my mother answered the door, I was standing right beside her because, …well, because it was Charlie. It was well known that Charlie was a legend not only in Sault Ste. Marie, but around the entire Eastern Upper Peninsula and beyond. He was an avid and very well accomplished hunter and fisherman, and I was always in awe of him whenever we had the opportunity to be together. He always takes time to talk to me, and that is far more important to young children than most adults even realize. Even at such a tender age, I idolized Charlie, not fully realizing that he would eventually become my teacher, my life coach, and my mentor. He was like a second father to me, and we had a special bond that was noted and admired by all who knew us well. Many of the lessons I would learn from Charlie were not about hunting or fishing, but instead, they were about people and about life.

Charlie and Dorothy Madigan

As my mother Josephine invited Charlie into our home, it seemed odd that he did not remove his red hunting coat, or his red Jones cap. In fact, he was still wearing his insulated red hunting pants and rubber boots while sitting at our kitchen table. He seemed excited. Immediately, I sensed that something was different. Something had happened that day and Charlie was looking for my dad, who was working that evening at my grandpa's store. Ely Andary & Sons was a men's fine clothing store in Sault Ste. Marie, Michigan, which was owned by my grandparents Ely and Marina Andary. Back then, most of the businesses downtown were open on Friday evenings until 9:00 p.m.

My Grandparents, Ely and Marina Andary.

My Father, Tony Andary at the Deer Camp, "the Lodge".

My mother offered Charlie a beer, and he gladly accepted, lighting a fresh cigarette as he began to describe the exciting events of his day. He spoke in detail of how he had shot and wounded a huge buck late that morning. He had been sitting at a well-known hunting location called "The Rock" which was a large flat shale stone under a big spruce tree on "The Section Line" (a property boundary line) at our hunting property which we affectionately called "The Lodge".

Apparently, at about 11:15 a.m. that morning, Charlie stood up to stretch under the big spruce. He had ust lit a cigarette before starting the walk back to his car when he looked to his left and saw a huge 10- point swamp buck facing him on the edge of the Section Line. The buck was staring at him. The big-bodied deer was very dark, almost black, with a dark, monstrous rack and thick neck. As Charlie swung his rifle and touched off a shot, the big buck turned and jumped into the woods, headed East towards Charlie's vehicle which was about a half mile away.

After waiting for about forty minutes, Charlie began to track the big buck, finding blood and fragments of bone in the process. In fact, he pulled a four-inch piece of bone out of his pocket to show us, which added to the excitement in our kitchen as he told us his story. The big buck inevitably headed South towards Munuscong Bay (which means "Bay of the Rushes" in the Ojibwe Anishinaabe language)—a popular duck hunting mecca at that time, and to this day. Clearly, Charlie was excited to tell his deer hunting partner, my dad, about the big swamp buck so that they could make a plan to try to retrieve that wounded buck the next day. As I listened to Charlie tell his story, I was so excited that I could hardly stand it!

As Charlie opened a second bottle of beer, my mother offered me a small glass of 7-Up with ice and a small bowl of potato chips. Mom made the best homemade French onion chip dip, and this was a typical Friday night after-dinner treat for me and my two older sisters, Loretta and Patty. Of course, I was asking Charlie lots of questions about the big buck and the day's hunt under the patient but watchful eye of my mother. "Don't bother Charlie, honey" she would say. And Charlie would politely respond, "It's Okay Jo, he needs to learn about these things because he's going to be deer hunting with us someday". So that was the beginning of my journey, my avocation, and at times my addiction to chasing the wily whitetail deer.

When Dad arrived home from Grandpa's store around 7:30 p.m. (my grandpa let him go early, so Dad could head to deer camp since it was mid-season), Charlie's hunting story and our giddy excitement began all over again. With additional details and an intense conversation about how they were going to track and locate this buck, my mother fed tuna casserole to the eager hunters. When they were finished eating, my Dad hurriedly changed his clothes and grabbed his suitcase and duffel bag as he and Charlie headed off to The Lodge, our deer camp. The Lodge was a glorious old log hunting lodge filled with local taxidermy and exotic mounts from around the world, located on the North shore of the Bay. As my dad kissed my mom and me goodbye, Charlie scooped me up in his arms and said, "Don't worry Little Tone, you'll be coming with us some day" trying to comfort me. Frankly, we all knew that I was far too young to tag along on this trip, and although I tried to hide it, my frustration was obvious.

When the garage door closed, I ran to our living room and jumped up on the couch, standing in the window waving goodbye to my dad and Charlie as they pulled out of our driveway in separate vehicles. I was trying not to cry, but there were tears rolling down my cheeks as I watched them disappear into the darkness. A light snow had begun to fall.

"How about a little more pop and chips, honey?" My Mom whispered into my right ear from behind, lovingly attempting to comfort me. "Okay, Mom!!!" I said excitedly, as I jumped off the couch and ran up behind her on our way back out to the kitchen. "Someday I'm going to hunt deer with Dad and Charlie, Mom! Someday I'll be going with them!" I exclaimed. And so, it began…

THE PLAN:

At first light, my dad walked with hip boots to the shore area of Munuscong Bay to a high spot overlooking the marsh and the bay. That was the area and direction the wounded buck was headed when Charlie had left the blood trail the previous day. Big bucks would often utilize the shoreline, tag alders, bullrushes, and the 8-10-foot-tall elephant grass as their sanctuary, especially when they were wounded. The high spot offered an excellent vantage point so that my dad could see over the thick cover and view a larger area with his rifle in hand.

The long and short of it: they never found that big, wounded swamp buck that day, since Charlie eventually lost the blood trail. But Voilà ! While tracking that big buck, he jumped another beautiful 10- pointer which my dad shot at about 10:30 a.m. as it was following a doe across the marsh. With whitetail deer hunting— you just never know! You must always be ready!

Thus, even as a four-year-old I was hooked, and my journey to becoming an accomplished deer hunter had begun.

SAFETY FIRST:

I learned about gun safety and hunting safety at a very early age, starting when I was about five years old. As was customary in the day, we began to learn about gun safety with a BB gun, and later with a pellet gun (air rifle). In the Spring, Summer, and Fall, my friends and I would "hunt" squirrels, birds, and chipmunks, originally without much success (thank the Lord). My first firearm was a Stevens Over and Under with a .22 caliber rifle on top and a .410 shotgun on the bottom—both single shots. Charlie's youngest child, Russ, and I were the same age. We were dear friends growing up and are still dear friends to this day, as is his sister Patti McCasey. We began hunting partridge and rabbits under the trained, watchful eyes of our fathers, as did most kids back then. By the time we were ten years old, we were also duck hunting with our dads, and Fall soon became my favorite season of the year.

My first deer rifle was my Dad's Remington 742 Woodsmaster, a 30.06 semi-automatic, which I used to shoot my first five deer. Later, my dad bought himself a beautiful 30.06 Browning semi-automatic (BAR) with a 2-7 power Leupold scope. A few years later he gifted me an identical Browning that I continue to use today, now fitted with a more powerful 3-10 power Leupold scope and customized raised scope mounts. (The raised mounts were the result of us tracking Tim McCasey's wounded 32 pound bobcat years later-another great story!)

A BLIND OF MY OWN:

My first year of deer hunting with a rifle was 1967, when I was twelve years old. I sat along the shoreline marsh of Munuscong Bay with my dad near a spot known as Moorehead's Tree. There was not much action back then, and we only saw a few does and fawns that year. The second year, I sat at the same spot for most of the season, but I was alone from this point forward. Gone were the days of sitting on a deer blind with my Dad. Gone were the days of being ten and then eleven years old (Russ and me) with our .410s loaded with a slug, tagging along in search of a big buck on Thanksgiving weekend at the end of the season. Looking back, we were there to watch and learn, without posing much of a threat to any of the bucks in the area.

Tony building his blind. However, in the early Fall of 1969, I set out to find my OWN spot for a blind, and that I did. I ventured away from the shoreline where my dad always hunted and headed Northwest to the Wynn Trail. (For years, I thought it was named the "Wind Trail"). A fellow named Schmidt had built The Lodge as a hunting lodge for paying guests in the early 1900s, and most of the trails and hunting spots were named by him—long before my time. As I continued walking Northwest along the Wynn Trail, I came upon a clump of three birch trees near a bend in the trail as it rose out of the swamp and onto a small ridge. I suddenly remembered stories about how Charlie's brother, Hugh Madigan, used to stand at the base, in the crotch of those three birches. "This was it! This was Hughey's spot!" I excitedly whispered to myself. (Charlie always called his brother Hughey, not Hugh).

As I continued north, I noticed that part of the old logging trail had been widened into a staging area. This space was once used to store log piles, which were later picked up and hauled away by loggers. "Wow, what a perfect spot for a blind!" I thought to myself. "What a great location and vantage point. This is it!!" I mused.

As I cautiously made my way further North on the trail, I continually did 360-degree scans, turning my head constantly in search of the best site for a blind. As I neared the midpoint of the vintage staging area, I looked ahead to my right and lo and behold, there it was—a large cedar stump on the East side of the opening. It was the perfect spot for my new blind, my OWN blind!

Ultimately, that cedar stump would have a ¾" square plywood board lag bolted to it, with a silent swivel chair mounted on top. The base of this swivel chair would be covered with soft, pliable rugs to prevent any squeaking sounds caused by rubber boots touching the metal. The 7'x7' blind around the swivel chair would be made of all natural materials. It would have poplar framing covered top to bottom with thick spruce and balsam boughs, except for the 1" x 6" boards and multiple layers of tar paper on the roof. The blind would be dark inside, with slightly offset shooting holes to avoid detection. I eventually added thick poplar rifle rests to each of the four shooting holes, creating a turret-like setup. From this position, I could swivel and scan each direction, keeping an eye out for a big buck. The shooting lanes to the North, South, and West were already in place because of the logging on that ridge years ago. Eventually I would create a narrow shooting lane to the East, looking into the swamp behind my blind, so all directions would be covered.

BAITING—FOR ALL THE WRONG REASONS:

Let's face it—today, baiting for deer is a huge business throughout Michigan, and across much of the United States and Canada. Sugar beets, apples, carrots, and corn are hauled into the woods by the ton each deer season, providing a huge economic boon for farmers and retailers alike.

But back in 1969, "nobody" baited for deer around here. And if one was inclined to do so, you'd be on your own to figure it out, looking for sources and types of bait to use. Heck, I had never even HEARD of a sugar beet back then! Nonetheless, I was always looking for an edge or a way to crack the "Whitetail Code". Suddenly, I had an idea. "What if I put some apples on the ground on the edge of my shooting lanes near the deer trails that cross the North/South shooting lane? That way, if a buck comes along, it might stop long enough for me to get a shot!" I reasoned. "That will work!" I proudly proclaimed to myself. Accordingly, I picked apples for many hours around our neighborhood and decided to use them as bait for my new blind. I started baiting about three weeks before that deer season, and I figured that I was ready!

Little did I know that, really, I had it all wrong. It is well known that people now bait deer to attract the does, hoping that a big buck will follow a doe in heat so that the waiting hunter might get a shot.

Mature bucks generally don't come to bait in the early Michigan deer season, although younger bucks like yearlings (1 ½ years old) do so to a fault. This is especially true because the young bucks have just been kicked out of their family groups by the matriarch and as a result, they are very vulnerable. However, this and a great deal more whitetail knowledge was way beyond my comprehension and bandwidth back then.

OPENING DAY:

Finally! The Opening Day of Michigan's deer season has finally arrived. It is November 15, 1969, and I have been waiting for this day, this moment, for over ten long years. Although I'm only 14 years old, it seemed like it took forever to get here. As I sat on my own deer blind that I had proudly crafted and baited, the dim light of the waxing crescent moon cast a silvery glow over the dense forest around me. The air is crisp and cool. I can easily see my breath in the moonlight that is seeping through some shooting holes around the perimeter of my homemade blind.

It is deathly silent, except for the faint trickling of the little brook that snakes its way through the swamp behind my new blind. All is still, yet I am keenly aware that the dense woods around me are teeming with nocturnal wildlife. The deer should be moving today, and surely already are under the cover of darkness. As I calmly but eagerly wait for the first light of dawn, my young mind races with memories of tradition, deer tales, and the deep excitement that has fueled my love for the outdoors and hunting for as long as I can remember. The legends and tales passed down have shaped my connection to this moment, making it more than just a hunt—it's a part of who I am. It is OPENING DAY!!!

THE MOMENT OF TRUTH:

As dawn begins to break over the Munuscong Bay Watershed, thoughts of old sayings and deer tales, seep into my mind: "To Hit is History, To Miss Is Mystery"

I can hear my dad saying, always with a big grin and a laugh. The darkness is beginning to fade.

I can hear the following words as daylight creeps into the woodlands.

"How long is deer season?" My Grandpa used to say, as he would loudly snap his fingers. "SNAAPP… It's that long!!!!!!" meaning that in the blink of an eye or the snap of your fingers, your deer season could be over, for better or for worse, depending on the accuracy of your shot.

"Remember you only get one shot," kept going through my head.

"Ya gotta make that first one count!", as many before me had proclaimed in virtually every deer camp throughout the UP.

All the stories, all the lessons, and all the training in my young life had finally brought me to this morning, and soon to this Moment of Truth.

It is a beautiful opening day with cool temps and a sunny morning to boot. I can see squirrels scurrying around the area and birds darting from here to there. At about 8:15 a.m. a large male partridge walks out into the lane to the South, about 40 yards from my blind. By 9:00 a.m. I am ready for a snack, so consequently, one of the peanut butter and jam sandwiches in my backpack quietly makes its way into my stomach. This is perfect!!! It is so exciting to be here and yet, the real excitement has yet to begin.

About 9:30 a.m. and without warning, I hear a crashing sound out in front of me, off to my right. It is coming from the Northwest, and it is coming FAST! I swing the swivel chair to the right and shoulder my rifle, quickly positioning it out the North shooting hole. I quietly and carefully take the safety "OFF" as I peer into my rifle scope. I see movement on the left side of the trail, and suddenly THERE IT IS!!!!; a nice 6-point buck, stopped on the edge of the woods. I quickly put the crosshairs just behind his right front shoulder, and gently squeezed the trigger as I had been trained to do.

The buck spins and is gone in a flash, heading back where it came from. WOW! My heart is pounding as I hear the buck crashing through the woods, clearly heading away from me. Then the sound is different, and it becomes rather faint until finally, I hear the worst sound of all – the sound of silence. I put the safety "ON", take a few deep breaths, and wait, trying to calm my nerves and slow my heartbeat. It's time for a drink of water and some more deep breaths.

LESSONS LEARNED:

Although I originally planned to wait at least an hour before getting out of my blind, I decided at the 45- minute mark to go look for blood. I exit the blind and sneak quietly Northward up the trail keeping my rifle at the ready. I'm walking very cautiously, stopping to look for any movement after each step.

As I got to the spot where the buck was standing when I shot, I stop and carefully scan the ground, grass and twigs for any signs of blood. NOTHING! I keep telling myself to stay calm and to concentrate on the task at hand. The deer trail where the buck appeared is not very evident. It is not a very pronounced trail, and is most likely a "buck trail", one that is not used or frequented by does and fawns.

Feeling the need to move on, I slowly enter the thick woods and begin trying to follow what looks like the Buckbuck trail to the northwest. It is very hard to see, and it's even more difficult to follow. "Easy does it. Just take your time and go slow" I keep telling myself. "That's what you've been taught. Look for blood or hair, or any sign of where this buck is running" is playing in my head. "Be patient" I'm thinking, but I'm not really feeling it. I am moving along slowly, but with each step forward, my heart is sinking a litlte bit more. "What if I don't find this buck? What if I don't find any blood? STOP IT! Think positive! Keep moving…" keeps playing in my young head.

Then suddenly, and although I have not yet found any blood, I found the next best thing – gouges in the ground with overturned leaves showing hoof marks where this buck is running !!!!

This is the first time in my life that I am actually tracking a wounded deer by myself, and I am being guided by the deer stories, the articles I've read, and the teachings that are playing in my head as I look for any sign of… THERE! THERE! I see some drops of blood! "Stay Calm. Go Slow. Take It Easy." I keep telling myself as I follow the hoof gouges and drops or patches of blood for about 50 yards more. I again stop and scan the thick bush, finally resting my eyes on a small patch of white under a little group of balsam trees ahead of me. I scurry directly to that spot and THERE IT IS! My first buck, a beautiful 6-point on Opening Day! I immediately make the sign of the cross and thank the Lord out loud. A profound feeling of joy and excitement, and a unique type of relief that I have never experienced comes over me. I study this wonderful specimen from a short distance away to make certain that it is safe for me to move closer.

After a few minutes, I approach the buck from behind and poke it gently with my rifle barrel to make sure that it is dead. I proceed to dress out my first buck after having watched my Dad and Charlie do so on a couple of occasions, and all is going well, thankfully. With the deer heart in a red plastic bag for Charlie (He loves deer hearts with bacon), I cover the buck in balsam boughs and then walk back to my blind. What a day!! I hunt until dark, and then walk out to "The Circle" where our vehicles are parked. It is a gravel two track in the shape of a large rectangle that had been used as a logging road many years ago. Dad, Charlie, Russ, Tom, and Tim McCasey, Patti's fiancé, are there to congratulate me and to help with dragging this buck out to the Circle. Eventually, we load the 6-point onto my Dad's truck and head back to Jo Bo Do to celebrate, and for some much-needed rest.

George Andary (the day before he died) and Tim McCasey
with Tim's 32 pound bobcat. I have the mount

(L-R) George Andary, Ely's nephew from whom we bought our deer camp in 1968 (he had 3 sons Joe, Bob, and Don-"Jo Bo-Do"); Ely; Dad, my Great Grandfather John Boula Andary, and Dad's brother Paul Andary

That night at deer camp was a memorable one, as was the wonderful venison stew dinner, and salad with freshly baked bread that Mom had provided for us. I learned that Charlie's son Tom Madigan had jumped that 6-point buck while walking South on the Section Line that morning, a few hundred yards northwest of me. Luckily that buck eventually showed up at my blind, albeit without any help from those strategically placed apples. I also began to learn that humility is the better part of valor, and that very quietly celebrating whitetail success internally is the best way to do it. Sure, I was extremely happy and excited to shoot my first buck at a spot that I found on my own, and in a blind I designed and built largely by myself. Yet I also became aware, maybe keenly aware for the first time, that being humble about the entire experience made me feel good. It made me feel very content. Suddenly, I felt a sort of quiet confidence and independence within me that I had never known before. Thankfully, that realization would stay with me not only when hunting and fishing, but throughout my legal career, and throughout my entire life. Little did I know that evening that this would be the first of many, many bucks, along with even more hunting stories and tales of deer camp to tell. More importantly, these exciting experiences would come with a myriad of valuable life lessons taught, and learned, all along the way. Thanks, Dad and Charlie, for giving me and my family this and many more lifelong gifts to enjoy, and to share with those we love and cherish.

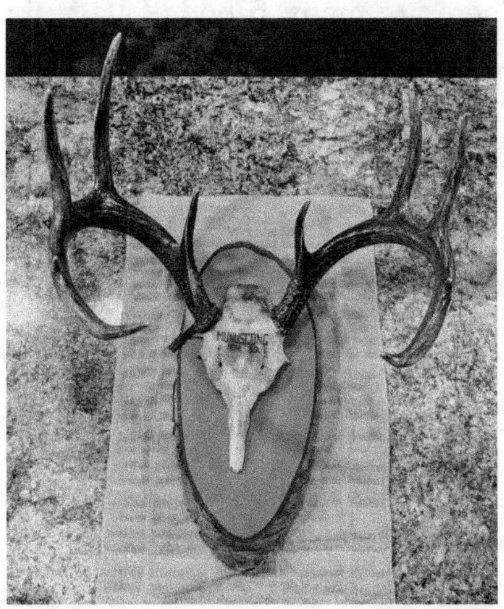

10 point my Dad shot while Charlie tracked the wounded swamp buck

CHAPTER 16

The Greatest Fishing In The World

THE SAULT RAPID'S AND THE ST. MARY'S RIVER.

By John McDonald

Do I consider myself a true fisherman? No, I consider myself a guy who loves to fish. There are many friends I have that are true fisherman and have a lot more knowledge about fishing than I do. My journey began fishing in the late 70s with my father in streams and small lakes. It wasn't until my best friend's Dad Eugene Porcaro took me fishing in a small 14-foot aluminum boat behind what we call the Power House. Which was the Edison Sault Power Plant back then. Fishing for white fish, trout, and salmon. That is where I fell in love with fishing.

HISTORY

As of 2023, the Soo hydropower plant is one of the oldest large generating stations still operating in the United States. The power canal and generator complex were begun in September 1898 and completed in June 1902, using engineering work from the first iteration of large-scale electrical generation in the late 1800s. It was from this work that the plant and utility that grew up around it acquired their historic name of Edison Sault, although Thomas Edison did not himself build the plant.

The Soo hydropower plant was built to contain 74 generators under a single roof. This was done under the constraints of the Classical style, by building an industrial structure of 1,340 feet (410 m) in length parallel to the St. Mary's River and facing the structure with masonry. The sandstone facing of the power station was chiseled out of blocks pulled from the Edison Sault Power Canal, the feeder canal that chutes water to the plant. President William Howard Taft visited the plant in 1911. The power canal and hydroelectric plant were together named a Historic Civil Engineering Landmark in 1983.

Although the hydroelectric plant could generate as much as 25–30 megawatts if operating at full capacity, grid planners rate it at 18 MW.

As I grew older now in my teens, I would ride my bike to the Power House with my soon-to-be lifelong friend Marty Porcaro. At the time in the early 80s there was a dock that ran along the St. Mary's river next to the powerhouse where freighters and large barges would dock. We would fish off of what we called that part of the Power House "the dock". You could walk along the dock and fish from shore. The dock ran approximately 450 feet. From the mid-80s to late 80s this was the spot to fish from shore for pink salmon and king (chinook) salmon. I spent countless hours fishing at the dock. During the day you could walk along the dock and see schools of pinks or chinooks. Back then you would see hundreds of pink salmon in a school at one time. You could almost pick the fish you wanted to catch. Pink salmon would average 1.5 to 2.5 lbs. The males could get up to 3.5 lbs. They were fun to catch, and you could catch them all day. My grandparents loved to eat them, so I would catch them 4 or 5 at a time and usually give the rest away, or we would sell them to tourists who would stop by to watch fishermen catch fish.

The older we got, we would be there from 10:00 p.m. until 8 a.m. We found that fish were biting best at night and early in the mornings. With glow-in-the-dark lures, we would sit on the dock and cast all night. Different fishermen would show up at 6:30 a.m.— 7:00 a.m. to fish, and we would sit in the best spots. Soon some guys would bring us donuts in the morning to hold them a spot on the dock. In the late 80s to early 90s it wasn't uncommon to catch 20–25 pound chinooks. When the salmon derby was going on there would always be big ones entered over 30 lbs. Boats would troll the St. Mary's River from the Government powerhouse or the Rock Cut in Barbeau. The more I fished for salmon the more I wanted to explore the rest of the river for more species of fish.

One of my many fishing stories is one with my Cousin Mike McCarthy and my great friend Cory Metro. Mike contacted me and said he was coming to town and would like us to get together and catch up. I haven't seen Mike in quite a while so of course I agree because 1, I haven't seen him in a while and 2, he is a great guy with great stories! I could sit and talk with him for hours listening to him tell stories of my father Donald (Mick) McDonald and the rest of our family.

Mike calls me and says he doesn't have a lot of time but would still like to see me. I told him that would be great and that we are going fishing. Well,, OK! He says! Knowing he didn't have a lot of time, he was in town to visit as many people as he could. I told him to meet us at Clyde's by the Sugar Island ferry, and we would pick him up on Cory's boat. I could tell, from the sound of his voice, he wasn't too sure of what to expect.

We pulled up in Cory's boat and Mike jumped in. Pretty sure this was a 1st for Mike, but we did it all the time. Away we go, getting set up to fish Chinook (King) Salmon. We were trolling in the St. Mary's River with bigger rods and J Plugs / Lures set to downriggers. Mike says I've never fished like this before. I said to him, "Well, let's see if we can't get you a fish." As we trolled and chatted about how each other had been. We get a release on one of the downriggers. Cory yells, "There's a fish! Grab it, Mike! Mike grabs it and sets the hook, the rod bends and the fight are on! Mike braces himself and the fish takes off.

The drag is whistling, Mike is holding the rod like a pro. The drag is set tight, and the fish isn't giving up that easily . Out of the water comes the fish, a big Chinook. "Did you see that, Mike yells"! The fish is not giving up and neither is Mike. Mike fights the big fish for about 15 minutes with Mike reeling the fish in for about 20 yards then the fish would run out for 15 yards. Back and forth until the big salmon does enough head shakes, gets off, and leaps out of the water. But just like that he was gone! I will never forget the look on his face when he grabbed that pole, and when the fish took off. I will also never forget the excitement that was in Mike's eyes. Mike might not have landed the big Chinook, but he got to experience one of the greatest experiences in the St. Mary 's River, the fight of a big Chinook salmon.

Mike grinned from ear to ear and talked about the fight of that Chinook from that point on until we dropped him back off in his car. I was so happy that I could be there with him to witness the experience that he just went through.

John loves ice fishing

The St. Mary's River drains Lake Superior, starting at the end of Whitefish Bay and flowing 74.5 miles southeast into Lake Huron, with a fall of 23 feet. For its entire length it is an international border, separating Michigan in the United States from Ontario, Canada

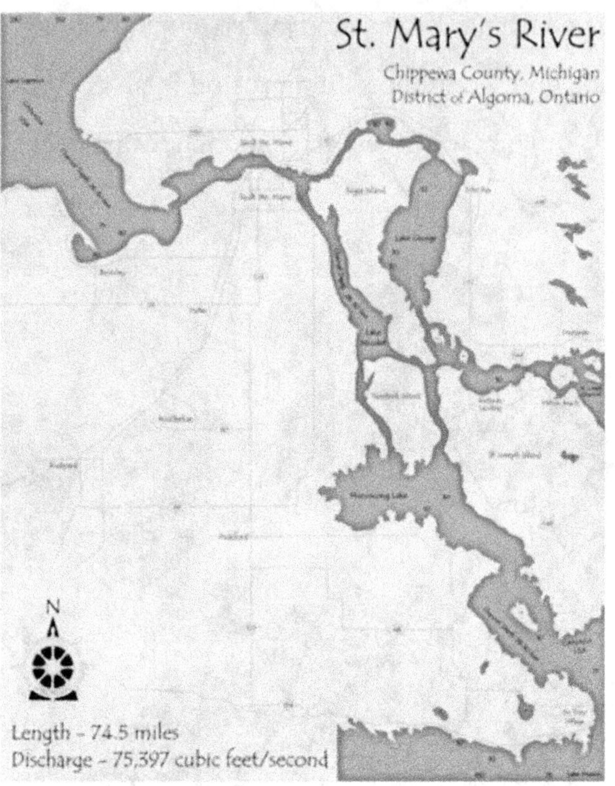

Fishing in the little bays along the river and catching large and small-mouth Bass, large pike to jumbo perch. Trolling for walleye around Sugar Island, Munoscong and the Raber Bay areas. I really liked catching walleye not only for the fight, but they became my favorite tasting fish to eat.

That's when I grew to love ice fishing. Fishing for walleye, pike, or perch and not knowing right away what is on the other end until it gets to the hole is excitement in itself. It may sound weird but catching fish through the ice on a little pole and light line is awesome! I have upgraded over the years to better ice shanties and a heater. But if you can have a nice calm sunny day and the fish are biting on the bay, there is nothing better. Not to mention the company you have with you.

One time while ice fishing on Munoscong Bay with a couple of my buddies Dan Gervasio and Kurt Hoopingarner, it was a beautiful day without a cloud in the sky and very little breeze. We have our poles in the holes fishing with a live minnow, hook with a bobber. My bobber goes under, I set the hook, and the fish takes off. The little rod bent, and the drag was whistling . The next thing I know is I have my two buddies coaching me or yelling at me. Don't horse it! Let it go! Be easy with it! Take your time! The next 5 minutes that it took to get the fish in seemed like 20 minutes of them yelling at me not to lose it. The fish ended up being a 26.5-inch northern pike. Not a huge pike, but a nice one. My personal best through the ice. Not sure if I had landed it if it wasn't for them coaching (yelling) at me. As the fish comes through the hole and onto the ice we start to celebrate. Because it was a team effort of course. In all the commotion and celebration I looked for my cellphone to take a picture, only to find that it had fallen off my chair and into the hole approximately 13 ft down. I went from super happy to pissed in 30 seconds. I went to my tackle box and searched for a lure that I thought I could hook it with. I wasn't too optimistic about getting it back, but I could see it. So, I thought I would try to get it back. As one of my ex-fishing coaches from 5 minutes earlier, Hoopy gave me flack and said I might as well kiss it goodbye, never gonna get it back!

Five minutes later I hooked it and brought it up to the surface. I yelled at my other fishing coach Dano, "I got it to come grab it when it gets to the top." I reeled slowly and Dano grabbed it. With that kind of luck, I should have bought a lotto ticket that day. We laughed and had another drink to celebrate both the fish and the return of my phone. We caught a couple of small perch after that. But what an awesome memory to have with two great friends on a nice winter day.

My next lesson was showing my son Ethan the sport that I grew to love so he could enjoy it as much as I do. From taking him to the fishing pond at rotary park next to the Sugar Island Ferry. Where the pond is stocked with different types of trout. To fish with my great friends Cory Metro and Darby McCoy for perch in Baie de Wasai. I took him with me any chance I could. It didn't take long before my son was hooked and fell in love with the sport of fishing. There is an old proverb that says, "The goal of the teacher is for the student to surpass the teacher." I couldn't agree more as when I got to witness it as my son started growing into a young man. A lesson that my fishing partner Dano and I discovered one day was not to underestimate the young and up-and-coming fisherman.

My son Ethan McDonald and his fishing partner Josh Lumsden. They have been friends since they were little guys, playing hockey and baseball together. Now fishing together for a few years, they were becoming better fisherman or just lucky. We set out for a last chance fishing tournament around Munoscong bay along the St. Mary 's river. As we got closer to the bay, my son informed me that they were going to fish for a different area of the bay than we were. I said keep us posted on how you guys are doing, and we will do the same. When we go ice fishing in a tournament around here, we usually stay all day from before the sun comes up to when the sun sets, and it's dark coming off the ice.

Dano says he has a spot, and we should do well. We get set up. We have one hole for a bobber and a minnow and 1 hole for jigging . We are about an hour into fishing, and I get a hit on my jigging pole. I set the hook to pull it out of the hole and it's a huge Perch. I look down at the hole and there is a school of perch swimming around down there. Our bobbers start to go under and it's chaos. Trying to catch as many perch as we can. There looked to be at least 25 of them when looking down the hole. After about 20 minutes of catching fish, re-baiting and untangling lines we caught 8 decent size perch or keepers and one big perch . I thought well that's good we're off to a good start. I also thought that perch could be on top of the leaderboard at the end of the day. About 20 minutes later I'm jigging and BAM!! I got a huge hit on my jig. I go to set the hook, my pole goes limp. I thought to myself I missed him and then BAM! Another hit I pull it again and my pole bends, and I have him hooked. The fight is on, and the coaching starts again from my fishing partner Dano. Easy, loosen the drag, DON'T HORSE HIM!! Let him go if he wants to go. The fight was awesome back and forth. I knew he was big, just not sure how big, and I didn't want to lose him. After a few minutes, that seemed like 10 but it was probably 2-3 I got him to the hole and Dano grabbed him. I had never caught that big of a Walleye through the ice. It weighed out at 5.5 lbs.

My new personal best. As we sit in our shanty for a few minutes after, I say to Dan, I sure do hope we out fish the boys today. He looks at me and starts laughing, looking at what we have caught already there is no way they are out fishing us. As my curiosity grew to wonder how the boys were doing, as they were fishing in a different area than us.

I sent them a message saying I'd caught a big perch and a five-and-a-half-pound walleye, and we had about 8–10 perch at the time. My son replies he's not doing too well, just a few here and there. But he did catch one big perch and thinks it's going to lead the tournament. Naturally, I respond that my perch is bigger, and then the trash-talking begins!

Dan Gervasio, Ethan McDonald, Josh Lumsden, and Jackson Gervasio. The boys beat their fathers in a great contest. New bragging rights are theirs now.

The day goes on, and we message back and forth, with him still saying his fish is bigger. We have to meet at the bait shop to weigh in the perch, so we will see. We don't have too much luck the rest of the day, we catch a few more keepers but nothing big. Ask them throughout the day and into the early part of the evening if they are having any luck. His response was little, few here and there. As our day concluded, we met up at the bait shop to weigh in. I got there first and weighed in. Now in my defense my perch was a bucket in our shanty which is warm from the heater we have. My perch weighed in at .69 and was in 3rd place at the time. Other anglers are bringing their fish in, and I get bumped to 6th. I'm texting my son that he only has a few minutes to weigh in, so he better get there quickly . He walks in the bait shop grinning ear to ear. Pulls out his perch, they set it on the scale, and it's .79. That is a big perch, and a lot bigger perch than mine. He takes the lead after the 1st day and is super excited! As am I that he is the leader, and I am still on the leaderboard. I give him a hug and must eat crow for a little while, but am super proud.

We walk outside to get in the vehicles to leave, and he says to me, let's go back to Dan's and clean the fish. I said, "Well there isn't that many, so it won't take long. So, sure!" He says, we got a few more in my truck. I said I thought you said you weren't having too good of luck. He says, well, we got a few later (with a shit eating grin on his face! I tell Dan that Ethan wants to go to his house and clean what we have because we are heading out again in the morning to fish. Dan agrees and we head to Dan's . I mentioned that they might have more fish than us on the way there. Dan says no way. We get to Dan's house and unload our fish on a table in his garage. Then earns the youngsters with their day's catch. I was shocked! I looked at Dan and said, I told ya! He looked at me and started laughing. Over the next hour and a half, we cleaned the fish and told stories of the day. That's when I learned my boy had become a fisherman.

Ethan and his catch— Beautiful Atlantic Salmon!

I am so glad that I was introduced to fishing at an early age. I am also glad that I introduced fishing to my son at an early age. The people you meet, the memories you get. Sometimes good, sometimes not so good. But most times there is always a positive that comes from a day's fishing. Especially nowadays, it seems younger people are more drawn to video games than spending time outside and enjoying nature.

Nowadays, I get to be the guest when I go fishing with my son Ethan McDonald and his friend Josh Lumsden. These young men are growing up in one of the greatest areas to fish in the United States. They are becoming great fishermen and study weekly on how to improve their fishing adventures. They are always fishing in different spots, checking in with other friends, and are watching videos on how they can improve and become a better fisherman. I love the fact that they never give up and are always changing baits, different lures, flies, colors, plastics and crank baits if they are not catching something. They aren't afraid to travel wherever they think they will catch fish. I believe within a few years they will become fishing guides themselves on the St. Mary's River.

Ethan's "Catch of the Day".

CHAPTER 17

The Bawdy Ballads from Dad

Some of my Father's greatest friends were Bill Murphy and the second was a man called Ernie Lee. Of course, stories and songs from Bill & Ernie seemed to be non-stop when they were all sharing a bottle of MacNish Scotch Whiskey. Bill especially loved to sing and recite poetry forever. Ernie loved to tell stories but would sing every song that Bill and Dad would sing. I called them the three musketeers. I enjoyed my time with them as I found them all a bit crazy but very entertaining. All three of them were raised in Irish families, so they had a common sense that each of them understood. Both Bill and Ernie were raised in camps with hard working men, in mining, and lumber. That's where they picked up their music. Their stories would keep you glued to your seat. Dad learned from Pop and Ma (his parents) several Irish and lumberjack songs, and he sang them at home. For my sisters, he sang a special song for each daughter. For Mary, he sang, 'The Rose of Tralee,' and for Kathy, he sang, 'My Lovely Rose of Clare.' But he did pick up some lovely Irish tunes from some Australian Navy friends he made during World War II. Dad was stationed in New Guinea and the Philippines, and it was there he learned Irish music, which the Australians sang back home in their pubs. And it wasn't Bing Crosby or Dennis Day. It was real Irish singers, like Joseph Locke and

John McCormick. Some of those who are reading this book is saying, why Australia? Many of you may recall that Australia was originally founded to be an Irish Penal Colony. So, if you were arrested in Ireland by the British Constabulary for being disorderly, causing civil havoc, or even stealing a loaf of bread, you were shipped to Australia and you had free passage. So, like the U.S. and Canada, Australia has a very large Irish population. That's how Dad learned his music. His favorites were The Wild Rover, The Moonshiner, and Enniskillen Dragoons. But I thought the best was the Australian favorite 'Waltzing Matilda.' The boys and he loved singing together the song about Irish soldiers going off to fight in the Spanish Civil War, the song was called 'Enniskillen Dragoons'. I later heard it sung in an Irish pub, in Cork City, and I was surprised some thirty years later how well Dad got it.

Enniskillen Dragoons verse -

Fare thee well Enniskillen, fare thee well for a while

And all around the borders of Erin's green isle

And when the war is over we'll return in full bloom

And we'll all welcome home the Enniskillen Dragoons

Our troop was made ready at the dawn of the day

From lovely Enniskillen they were marching us away.

They put us then on board a ship to cross the raging main,

To fight in bloody battle in the sunny land of Spain.

The songs 'Wild Rover' and the 'Moonshiner' were simply drinking songs but cleverly worded and a great little story to each. There was a great verse in each tune, I enjoyed watching the faces of Bill and Ernie,

Wild Rover verse -

I went into an ale house, I used to frequent

And I told the landlady, me money was spent.

I asked her for credit,

She answered me nay,

Such a custom as yours, I could have any day.

And it's no, nay never,

No nay never no more, Will I play the wild Rover, No never, no more.

The Moonshiner verse -

I'm a rambler I'm a gambler I'm a long ways from home

And if you don't like me, well leave me alone

I'll eat when I'm hungry, and I'll drink when I'm dry

And if moonshine don't kill me, I'll live till I die

As I look back at it now, I'm smiling and enjoying the memories of those wonderful times. I see Bill, his golden tooth shining as he sings with that huge Irish smile. Then there's Ernie, serious and focused, making sure he gets the words right before loudly belting out when he knows he's nailed them. And Dad, singing softly the songs Bill and Ernie liked, but strongly singing the Enniskillen fight song. These were great songs and in our lifetimes, we sang them hundreds of times. The one he sang with the greatest Australian accent; however, was the tune, Waltzing Matilda. It was a great song. When they sang it, you knew each of them enjoyed the story and then singing the chorus was special, listening to the three trying to harmonize.

Down came a jumbuck to drink at that billabong

Up jumped the swagman and grabbed him with glee

And he sang as he stowed that jumbuck in his tucker bag

" You'll come a Waltzing Matilda with me "

Waltzing Matilda, Waltzing Matilda

You'll come a Waltzing Matilda with me

And his ghost may be heard if you pass by that billabong

" You'll come a Waltzing Matilda with me "

These were the songs Dad learned from the Australian sailors during the war. But the song he learned as a boxer himself, was about the Irish heavyweight fighter named John Morrissey. My brother John and I loved that song and sang it with Dad. It was Dad's way of telling us it doesn't matter how big or small you are, it's your heart that matters and to never give up.

BRAVE MORRISSEY.

The Irish boxer.

The Russian heard of Morissey,

He had a dreadful punch.

But now one stood a chance you see

when the Russian started to box.

He hit our own dear Morissey

and flattened him to the floor,

and just before the count of ten

he sprang up for more.

When upped jumped brave ole Morissey,

With a heart so big and true,

and Morissey with his dreadful blow,

he broke the Russian's heart.

Morissey hopped around the ring, and waved toward the crowd,

and passed the Russian champion still laying on the ground.

You know, I was the fortunate one. To experience these folks telling stories of their youth and then singing as if there was no tomorrow. It was a very special moment, and I was a part of it.

CHAPTER 18

The Settlement At Tone, And The Secret Oaths Of The KKK

As you drive toward Pickford, on M-129, passing through what was once the settlement of Ransonville, you come up to the Blinking light to turn onto Tone Toad. Going west, the road passes through Kincheloe, and onto Kinross Township.

But beginning at that turn on Tone Road, going South to Pickford where their old Community Park was, and on land that is the Golf Course today, was a settlement known as Tone. Just 2–3 miles outside of Pickford. Our great-grandfather Thomas Hassett named the settlement in honor of Theobald Wolfe Tone— an Irish rebel and martyr for Irish freedom. Thomas was the son of Thomas Hassett and Mary O'Connor. They were married in Limerick where Thomas, his older brother Michael, and his younger sister Julia lived until they moved the family to Ennis in County Clare. In Tone, Michigan, a number of Irish Catholic immigrants were arriving and homesteaded there and settled with their families. Hassett and two other residents, John T McCarty and John MacDonald, signed the original application for a Post Office, and in

1897, it was established. The Post Office continued its service through 1917, when Thomas died. The Post Office relocated to Kinross in 1917 where my cousin, Eva Hassett, took charge as Postmaster. She was the granddaughter of Thomas Hassett, the postmaster and Irish patriot.

Thomas Hassett, postmaster of Tone, great-grandfather, IRB member

He came to the Pickford area in 1879 with his wife, Bridget McMahon, and his older brother, Mike. They each homesteaded 160 acres of land. They built their homes from Poplar logs, and with his six children began to clear the land. They were proud farmers.

Other Irish settlers followed, including the Halls, the Lawlesses, the McSweeneys, the McCarthys, the O'Callaghans, the Donnellys, the Hendersons, the Campbells, the Duggars, and the Doyles. Many others arrived during those immigration years and up through 1920. He had a very interesting history, as a young man in his late teens working as a farm laborer in West Clare he took an oath to join a secret organization known as the Irish Republican Brotherhood, (IRB). This was an outlawed organization in Ireland, known to be radical enemies of British rule in Ireland, or in today's jargon a Terrorist. According to English law, he was a terrorist. Here was the Oath he took,

THE IRB OATH OF GRAMPA HASSETT

'I, Thomas Hassett, do solemnly swear, in the presence of Almighty God, that I will do my utmost, at every risk, while life lasts, to make Ireland an independent Democratic Republic; that I will yield implicit obedience, in all things not contrary to the law of God ['laws of morality'] to the commands of my superior officers; and that I shall preserve inviolable secrecy regarding all the transactions ['affairs'] of this secret society that may be confided in me. So, help me, God! Amen.'

From age 18-22 he did his best to annoy, disrupt, and create enough trouble and violence to get noticed by the British police force in Ireland. He never harmed anyone, but according to the story passed down, he and his mates got hold of some gunpowder to do some blasting. They were caught setting it up just before the explosion of a British government building. So he was arrested, and his sentence was to be sent to Australia, the penal colony, or sent off to Dublin to Kilmainham Jail to be hanged . He was arrested in Ennis and placed in a makeshift jailhouse and his mates broke him out, and immediately put him on a boat to Wales in the Western part of England. So, Thomas was to hide out and work in the Welsh coal mines.

Wales was a perfect choice as it too was a Gaelic Country and welcoming to the Irish cause over the years. He worked in the coal mines of Wales and changed his name for a few years to Blennerhassett, a strong English name. He sent for Bridget, and the two were married in 1862. As years passed, He was now a married man with young children, and luckily for him, the past did not catch up with him. It wasn't until the 1870s when his brother Mike, a bachelor, first came to Chippewa County and the idea of owning his own land to farm was very appealing. He returned to England, and it took just one year to be convinced enough for Thomas to take the ship with his entire family to Goderich, Ontario, Canada. From there, he and Michael sailed to Sault Ste. Marie, hired two horses, and went up the Old Mackinac Trail. Off they went to the land they were to Homestead. Michael had built a cabin on site, but the roof was unfinished. Once that was done, Thomas sent for his family, and The Hassett's have landed.

As I reflect on him as a young man and the secret oath he took, I compare it to the oaths taken to join groups like the Orange Order, the KKK, or the Masonic Lodge with their 33rd Degree Master Mason. At that time in our country, religion really drove the agenda of our country's social structure. The Catholics of course had their own counterparts, first the Knights of Columbus, with its four degrees. The 4th Degree K of C knight has similar threads to that of the 33rd degree Master Mason. The difference was one was Protestant, while the other a Catholic. Then came the AOH— the Ancient Order of Hibernians. This was the body equivalent to the Orange Order but this one for Irish Catholics. But I've come to believe the Oath taken by the KKK still lives in parts of our country today— STILL.

Their oath — I solemnly swear, in the presence of Almighty God, that I will never reveal the name of the person who initiated me, that I am not now a member of [any organization] whose aim and intention is to destroy the rights of the South, or of the States, or of the people, or to elevate the negro to a political equality with myself; and that I am opposed to all such principles, so help me God."

For instance, I didn't know of the resurgence of the KKK as an active organization in 1915. But it reached Michigan, and across the UP, you could hear the old folks sharing stories. In the early twenties, the KKK UP headquarters was located in Manistique, Michigan. Their purpose was to uphold the moral fiber of the nation, and spread quickly across the Upper Peninsula due to heavy European immigration, of which a greater number were Catholic. They espoused the tenets of temperance, and prohibition became one of its major issues, with the strict enforcement becoming one of its leading issues. Even the editor back then of the Sault Evening News was quoted as saying, "The Klan was encouraging patriotism, and since the United States is a free country, there could be no objection to the group and its goals." Most other editors in the UP, took a very anti-Klan position and saw it as an un-American organization.

Around 1915, during the nadir of American race relations, the Ku Klux Klan began promoting a conspiracy theory claiming that Fourth Degree Knights swore an oath to exterminate Freemasons and Protestants. The

Knights of Columbus vehemently denied the existence of any such oath, calling the rumors libel. In 1923, the Knights of Columbus offered $25,000 to any person with proof that the fake oath attributed to the fourth-degree membership was part of any authentic ceremony. The Knights began suing distributors for libel in an effort to stop this, and the KKK ended its publication of the false oath.

In Chippewa County, stories surrounded the KKK's involvement in disruption in our towns, and villages where Catholic immigrants were strong in numbers. They became quite large of course in Detroit and grew to be quite big. Big Rapids, for example, was a target, where high numbers of blacks lived. But in the North, it was aimed at Immigrants who were Catholic. So, if you were Polish, Irish, Italian, French, or even German during the years after WWI, the KKK were mostly heard from and left their scars among many people.

In Michigan and the UP, the second incarnation of the Ku Klux Klan was from 1905 to 1930 . It frequently referenced the USA's 'Anglo-Saxon' blood, echoing 19th-century nativism. While most KKK members believed they upheld American values and Christian morality, virtually every Christian denomination officially denounced the Ku Klux Klan. That was also the case in Chippewa County!

So, it was in 1919, one lovely autumn evening with my grandmother and her older Sister Annie sitting on the front porch with my Aunt Doine, a little two-year-old baby. Up drove three men with their white hoods, holding a cross they burned and a sign that said, "GO HOME! "

My Grandmother, Julia Hassett McCarthy

I'm sure the women were scared as it was just the three of them. The men of the family were all gone, but my grandmother grabbed a shotgun from inside the farmhouse, and my great Aunt Annie grabbed a spade shovel. And both women chased after the three as their car took off. Soon afterward, a Catholic church in Pickford, the Church of The Sacred Heart, in the center of the Orange Order for Chippewa County, was razed to the ground. Built in Pickford in 1890, The Church of the Sacred Heart was founded by Jesuit missionaries, Father Chartier and Father Dulude . Father Dulude was very special in my family as he cured my grandmother, Julia Hassett of the rheumatoid arthritis she had as a child. The church burned in 1919, reportedly from a cinder of a garage fire nearby. Nothing was ever proven as to a crime, and no charges were ever issued, but the feelings are still present even to this day. The St. Joseph's statue was saved from the fire by a Mr.

Quinnell. It sits today in Holy Family Church in Barbeau. It all starts with those secret oaths in a way, doesn't it?

The Klan marching down Front Street in Marquette, 1926

Church Of The Sacred Heart

This Church of The Sacred Heart was built in Pickford in 1890 on the corner of Main Street and the Meridian, facing north. Father Chartier S. J. was the missionary in this area when the church was built through his efforts. Father Du Lude S. J. was also a very active missionary in the area. These priests were Jesuit Missionaries of whom Father Gaunier was one of the last. The above information was given by Rev. Oliver O'Callaghan The church was destroyed by fire in 1919. The origin of the fire is uncertain but many believe a cinder from a garage that burned the same night perhaps caused the destruction of the Church of The Sacred Heart. The fire had made great headway when noticed and it is said the first arrivals at the scene broke the door down and carried a little of the contents out in the church yard and later carried these to a blacksmith shop on the east side of the Meridian (Hugh Carr's shop).

A statue that was in the Pickford church is at present in The Holy Family Church at Barbeau having been carried from the burning building, it is said, by John Quinnell. Rev. Fr. Gagnier said Mass here Sunday morning, April 16, 1908.

CHAPTER 19

When The Us Military Bases Were King In Chippewa County

The military was certainly King of the Chippewa County economy from the 1930 s to the 1970 s. The city certainly had a large industrial base as well, at least on through to the end of the 1950s, but the military impact on our overall culture, not just the Socioeconomics of the town, was huge. One of the greatest memories I will always have is seeing our old boys from WWI march in our July 4th parade. They were our Drum and Bugle Corps, and each of them played some form of musical instrument, but each of them served on the lines in France and there in the trenches. At least four of them were gassed by the Germans and had the scars to prove it. They all were our heroes. The Sault had a great reputation of Patriotism, and being a recipient of five military bases, thousands of our citizens signed up to serve in our country's Armed Forces.

Kincheloe AFB

Sault 753rd Radar Squadron

37th Missile Squadron

Defense spending generates jobs directly and can improve economic output indirectly through the spillover of technology and human capital to the civilian economy. However, defense spending also has opportunity costs because it diverts resources from government programs that might do more to promote growth. I would bet there wasn't one town, village or unincorporated area of our County that wasn't benefited by the dollars spent by the military services personnel at those bases. Let alone the hundreds of civilians employed at the bases.

Here was the line-up of bases, the Air Force had the largest number of Service personnel and employed the most citizens throughout our communities and county. The Kinross Air Base was the largest. It was later renamed after an Air Force test pilot, Ivan Kincheloe, was killed. The Base remained part of the Strategic Air Command and Bombing Squadron. The base itself was a large, 4,000-acre facility and a self-sufficient military development. It closed in the later part of the 1970s. The next was another Air Force component, called the 753rd Air Radar Squadron. It, too, closed down in the later part of the 1970s. It was located just outside the city limits, and although they had barracks for personnel on base, the majority of personnel lived throughout the county and city. The final Air Force facility was placed strategically in RACO, the former large sawmill named after its investors, the Richardson and Avery families. It's located near Brimley, out on the plains with that great sandy soil. The large mill closed in the 1920s. A new 37th Missile Squadron was placed there, and it served under the direction of Kincheloe AFB, with its mission to protect the Soo Locks. It closed in the early 1970s. The U.S. Army had a semi large station after the close of Fort Brady toward the end of WWII again to protect the Soo Locks. A newly established base called Camp Lucas was developed near Fort Brady. Its location was strategic, right in the middle of the Ashmun Hill area of Sault Ste Marie. By 1960 the base's closure had a great impact on the economy, and as I mentioned its location was right in the middle of the city.

Finally, the U.S. Coast Guard has had all its bases in the Sault for years and has had a major presence for years in the city. It still remains to this day.

X

U.S. Coast Guard Base—Sault

Camp Lucas - Sault

We were so fortunate in the Sault to have this military presence. We have certainly bounced back economically from their closures, but it left a permanent commitment woven into the Sault fabric. Furthermore, we take great pride in knowing our country is the vanguard of Democracy, and our town is deeply committed to the defense of our country. I've believed since my Dad used to bring me as a young boy, to Camp Lucas and listen to the evening taps, with my Dad saluting the lowering of our nation's flag, Patriotism is our forte.

CHAPTER 20

Hallesy's Bar

Years ago, when I was at the EDC in Chippewa County, I was in Chicago and its suburbs making three company visits. All had indicated an interest in setting up at the former Kincheloe Air Force Base, and I was on the next plane to see them. We drove into Naperville to have a great lunch at their beautiful golf course. There I met several folks coming in for their lunch after their game. One was a gentleman in his sixties, who wanted to chat with me when he found out I was from Sault Ste. Marie Michigan.

Apparently during the 1950s, he was a sales Rep who routinely visited the Soo as one of his large clients in his chemical business was our own Union Carbide.

He was very entertaining, and we enjoyed the visit. I was helping him catch up on our life since his 20-year absence with our Carbide plant's closing. But I will never forget his description of the Soo. He loved going there, he said, "but it really is a town of churches and saloons on every corner, and ice rinks everywhere". But he said, "You have some of the finest people I've ever met."

I didn't take exception to his statement, as it was his opinion, but I did say, "I'm happy our town and Union Carbide provided him a good living."

As I thought of it then and do so again today, the Sault has had a colorful history, and we did have several churches and a variety of places to enjoy a drink. In fact, he was right, as driving around the Soo in the 50s, we had a skating rink and hockey rink in almost every neighborhood.

We had some wonderful hotels with entertainment to enjoy a nice dinner and drink, and dancing. We had the Ojibwe and the old Park Hotel, the Brunswick, the Belvedere, the Delmar, and the Hickler.

They all were popular Places to eat like Taffy Abel's, the Antler's, the Penthouse, and drinks were also served. Then we had our Private Clubs and Military Organizations like the Elks, the Moose Lodge, the VFW, and the American Legion. We had our Nightclubs like the Northview, then we had our Bars and Saloons, each with its own customer base. We had the bomb shelter, the Majestic Bar, the Merchants, the Savoy, the Ship's Lounge. A few miles outside of town, we had two very nice establishments where you can enjoy a nice meal, have a nice drink and enjoy some dancing. Lazy Bob's and the Dafter Inn were great places to enjoy. But the two bars in my opinion that had some great historical significance were the Alpha Bar and Hallesy's Bar. Each was family owned and operated for three generations. One was Greek American and the other Irish American. I liked that.

Here is the story of one of those Bars, my favorite—Hallesy's, and how it came to life in the 1930s, and the three generations of the Irish family who operated it.

HALLESY'S BAR

By: Barb Hallesy Wirt May 23, 2024

The history of Hallesy's Bar begins with Patrick Hallesy, my paternal great-grandfather, and his wife Catherine Neville Hallesy. They emigrated from County Cork, Ireland, to southern Ontario, Canada, where they got married and had four sons. One of these boys was my grandfather, Thomas Patrick Hallesy. Another brother died in childhood. His mother couldn't cope with the loss and entered a mental hospital, where she spent the rest of her life.

Patrick Hallesy died when my grandfather was 16 years old, and the brothers went their separate ways after several years under the care of a housekeeper. Thomas occasionally heard from his brother, Dennis, later in life.

In 1905 census records, Thomas Patrick was living in Sault Ste. Marie, MI, and working as a bartender at the Sherman House. The border between Canada and the United States was more fluid in those days, and when he registered for the draft, Thomas claimed to have been born in Milan, MI. We found no records to corroborate that claim.

Laura Horton, a red-haired farm girl from Goderich, Ontario, worked as a waitress at the Sherman House. Her family had moved to the Dafter area, and she and Thomas were married in 1906. I recall her referring to Grandpa as "a gay blade," which in the parlance of the day meant that he was handsome and charming.

Laura converted to Catholicism for her Irish Catholic husband and raised their ten children in that faith. I don't think my grandfather was ever as steadfast in the Church as Grandma was. All of their children referred to them as Ma and Pappy.

Thomas supported his growing family as a cook in a lumber camp and on a steamship until he acquired a small grocery store during Prohibition. I believe he sold "hootch" from the back room of the grocery store. The desire to be a saloon keeper was always there.

I never knew my grandfather because he was leaving this world when I arrived. My mother loved him and said he spoke with a heavy Irish brogue. My Aunt Laurel Hallesy Trim, his youngest child, remembers walking downtown with him when she was a wee girl. Often, someone down on their luck would ask her Pappy if he could spare some money. Thomas never failed to help anyone in need. Yet, he had a melancholy side to his gregarious personality and would occasionally take to his bed with a bottle of whiskey and demand more until he was extremely sick from alcohol. Then the binge would end, and he would get on with life until whatever daemon within him required another bout of drinking.

In 1937, he opened the Lakeview Hotel. It was a saloon and rooming house, and there was no lake view on Ridge St. The whole family also lived upstairs in Lakeview as they married and left home.

According to Aunt Laurel, it was a rollicking abode where she grew accustomed to being teased and protected by her older brothers.

My grandmother tended to the children and the cooking. As a farm girl, she wasted nothing. She loved hunting, fishing, and gardening. She taught her kids to cook Thanksgiving dinner because she couldn't miss the first day of deer season. I remember a news article proclaiming her the first person to bag a buck one year. She and my grandfather were well-matched and welcomed all the spouses joining their children in that big family.

Uncle Dutchie worked at Lakeview with Pappy so he and their Ma could travel. He died unexpectedly at their cabin on the lower St. Mary's River. The siblings remained a close and loving family all their lives. I remember enjoying visits to the Lakeview with my dad when we were walking to the Locks in the summer. My Uncle Dutchie Hallesy and Aunt Marie (Pingatore) Hallesy replaced my grandfather as proprietors after Pappy died. There was a long bar in the main room where men stood (no stools), and there were spittoons. I stayed far away from them! But there was also a grand jukebox with lights and endless musical choices. Men at the bar always gave me money to play the Nickelodeon. I could barely make out the selections. When my mother questioned the wisdom of taking me there, my dad said it was good reading practice.

Years later, my mom stopped bar visits when my little sister drank her milk like a bar patron would throw back a shot of whiskey. By then, I was old enough to recognize the move and know that my mother would not be amused.

In 1958, my Uncle Dutch moved his business to the Moose Lodge Building at 730 Ashmun Street. It was an imposing three-floor red sandstone building. Aside from the Moose Lodge, it housed a paint store, fourteen apartments, and Hallesy's Bar. It was a lovely, welcoming little bar. I recall a dog theme with a mural on one wall. Behind the bar, there were mirrors and colorful neon lighting. Hallesy's was always an Irish saloon, but not overly so. My dad and uncle were quietly Irish and did not need to proclaim their ethnicity. Like all taverns in our hometown, the business took a positive upswing when a new lock was under construction. My uncle's business was quite successful.

On the other hand, my dad, Frenchy Hallesy, had moved to Milwaukee with the Northwest Leather Company when the tannery closed in the Sault. My mother was not inclined to uproot her girls and her dependent mother to move to Milwaukee. It was too far for my dad to get home as often as he wanted, so after a year or two, he came back. He was in his late fifties and had worked at the tannery for almost thirty years with no retirement benefits. He had to find a job, so he worked as a custodian at the International Bridge and the Federal Building and did a night shift for my uncle at Hallesy's Bar.

In 1962, we heard many sirens while I was at an evening skating party at Mary McCarthy's outdoor rink. Fires were frightening in my hometown because of the many old buildings. We all rushed to see what was burning. It was the Moose Lodge Building, with Hallesy's Bar included. I saw my dad and uncle looking pale and horrified and knew this was a disaster. There would be nothing left to fix. Uncle Dutchie started again in a modest storefront building at the other end of the same block at 718 Ashmun Street. It was less classy than the last bar. Still, it was the same long bar with a bowling machine, a pool table, and some booths in the back to accommodate the weekly cribbage league that moved from bar to bar. Before my uncle died in 1968, he offered to sell the business to my dad.

It was a challenge that required a bank loan and help from my mom's sister. Her husband, my Uncle Steve Wood, was a rum runner between America and Canada during Prohibition. He kept all his ill-gotten gains in a suitcase, where it remained for all the years they lived in Florida. They lived simply in a trailer park where Uncle Steve did repairs, and Aunt Ceil cleaned motel rooms. She returned to her hometown after Uncle Steve died. God bless her for offering some of these suitcase savings to my dad for part of the bar down payment forty years later…cash from a suitcase under the bed! If you're wondering how two Irishmen were nicknamed Dutchie and Frenchy, it came about when they were young altar boys, and the priest couldn't tell them apart. Gorden and Francis were dubbed Dutchie and Frenchy. My dad was okay with that because he didn't like having a name that could also be a girl's name.

At this point, I was a student at Northern Michigan University in Marquette, majoring in Social Science, and feeling a need to get out of the Upper Peninsula and save the world while exploring. I joined Volunteers in Service to America (VISTA), the US alternative to the Peace Corps. It was a one-year commitment to live on a subsistence wage in service to areas of extreme poverty. I trained at the Jane Adams Center in Chicago for my assignment to the two poorest counties in the Appalachian Hills of Ohio along the Kentucky border. It was my first experience in a city of such size with fellow volunteers from around the country in the tumultuous year of 1968. I met young radicals like the Chicago Seven organizing for social change. I also met charismatic leaders like Martin Luther King Jr. The whole year was a life-changing experience for the Catholic schoolgirl who had not even left

UP for college. Likewise, I worked through a Community Action Agency, part of President Johnson's War on Poverty. It was community organizing on the ground level, which was excellent work for young idealists like me.

At Hallesy's Bar, Frenchy was ready to retire after two hip replacements and two open-heart valve replacement surgeries at the Mayo Clinic in Rochester, MN. I returned to help him at the bar when my VISTA year ended. I started working the late-night shift while he worked days. People my age were coming home from VietNam and returning to school or work. Several groups of them were regulars at Hallesy's. It had always been a working man's bar, a gathering place for the union trades of two generations, older folks in the neighborhood, and many men who stopped by for a beer now and then. It was a safe haven for chronic alcoholics, who would cash their disability checks and entrust the money to my dad, keeping it in an envelope to protect it from theft and from themselves, so they wouldn't spend it all on drinking too quickly. I continued that when I took over the bar. Their money was safe with us, even though they never spent a dime in the bar. It all started with Pappy, who opened his wallet and shared what he had with anyone in need. The Irish term Anam Cara, roughly translated as soulmate, comes to mind when I think of the familiar faces I saw every week in that bar and how kind they were to each other. It was like the television comedy series Cheers, where "Everybody knows your name, and everyone's glad you came."

I don't want to imply that there was never any discord among my customers under the influence of alcohol. I particularly remember the bachelor party of a fellow Loretto alumnus. All was going well until I looked up from drawing a beer and saw the whole crew slowly throwing punches at each other like actors in a silent movie. I had to come from behind the bar and send the hooligans out with threats of calling the police.

Bea Pemberton was a barmaid who worked for years at Hallesy's. She was a sweet lady, well-loved by everyone, young and old. I never worried about Bea or any woman working there because most customers were respectful and loyal defenders of the barmaids. When Frenchy finally retired, I took over his day shift and did all the ordering and banking for him. I hired some new bartenders for the late shift. Some were great; some were not. If they were not great, word got back to me quickly, often with a phone call at home telling me to hurry and make a surprise visit to see what was happening. Bea was always stellar, dependable, and easygoing.

I consider my years at Hallesy's Bar to be an essential part of my life education. I entered that world as a know-it-all twenty-two-year-old woman. But I quickly learned to shut up and listen to people's stories because everyone had a story I could learn from. They taught me that respect is a two-way street between young and old, men and women, and rich and poor. It was a lesson that served me well in my work and life.

I learned that alcohol is powerful and highly addictive for many. Even my adored dad fell off the wagon when he and my Uncle Tom started drinking Tommy's homemade dandelion wine after many years of sobriety. Most of the Hallesy brothers were what I call payday alcoholics, hard-working men who were sober while working, but indulged in drinking on the day they were paid. I used to cash numerous plumber and electrician paychecks on Fridays. I learned that bartenders are like priests. People tell them things while drinking that should always remain in trusted confidence. Some stories are never shared.

In 1972, Mike Wirt finished grad school at the University of Michigan. We were married in the Loretto convent yard because, you know, Barb was still in her hippie girl phase. Father Monroe officiated, just as he had with my parents before my dad went to WWII.

Our honeymoon was driving across the country with a beagle and a U-Haul trailer to Spokane, WA, where Mike started his career with the Spokane County Library District, retiring as the director in 2012. I retired from Spokane Public Schools three years earlier. We've lived in Spokane for over fifty years now. Our son, Brendan, and his partner, Melissa, are Washingtonians. Our granddaughter, Kiera, will soon graduate from Washington State University. We're Gonzaga Basketball fans now, but we're still Yoopers at heart. We relish the icy mountain lakes and woods of North Idaho because they remind us of home.

That left the last and youngest Hallesy to manage Hallesy's Bar, my sister, Pam Hallesy Kaplan. She was only eighteen, so young to take on the responsibility of running a saloon. New younger people who were rowdier were coming in, and a few of the older generation were misbehaving in strange ways. She had her hands full. Bea was nearly retiring, and Pam hired a former Coast Guard member, Pete Peterson, a reliable, personable bartender. Her future husband, Ed Kaplan, also a Coastie, was a regular at Hallesy's Bar. His mother was Bea McCoy from Sugar Island. His dad met her while stationed at the Coast Guard base in the Sault. Pam still had the great guys who would step in if a barmaid needed help. Jim Gordon and Heck McKay were formidable men who nobody would ever challenge. God bless them. She also had help from one of my classmates, who I always think of as the guardian angel of Hallesy's Bar. Pat Murphy organized a winning basketball team for us to sponsor, and coached a women's softball team when Pam was managing. He was also a powerful protector, though sometimes he caused unacceptable fights over his girlfriend.

Pam kept helping my dad until he sold the business in 1974 to Fred Benoit, another Loretto graduate, who had become a successful restaurant owner in the Sault. Thus, Hallesy's Bar became The Gin Mill. Fred sold it in 1976 to Bob Allen, and it became Allen's Gin Mill. I believe my cousin Tony Hallesy worked for Bob Allen tending bar. Appropriately, the last Hallesy to work in that bar was Dutchie's only son.

John Granam bought it at an auction in 2014. The building now houses The Wicked Sister Bar and Restaurant, presently owned by Kathy Howell.

I always stop in when I'm back in our hometown. The Anam Cara spirit of our Irish roots remains in that old building, which I love visiting. I am trying to remember if there's still a jukebox, since food service requires more table space. I like to think that "Who Threw the Overalls in Mrs. Murphy's Chowder?" is still playing somewhere as it did in the Lakeview Hotel. The song I remember from Hallesy's Bar is the Beatles' "Hey, Jude." I blasted it every morning while prepping for the day.

Here's to everyone who ever stood at my grandfather's Lakeview Hotel Bar wondering where the lake was.

Here's to everyone who played a game of cribbage with my uncle or my dad at the first Hallesy's Bar that burned to the ground. And cheers to all who warmed a stool at the last Hallesy's Bar with my sister or me.

Thank you for fond memories from all the Hallesy's saloon keepers: Thomas Patrick, his sons, Dutchie and Frenchy, and his granddaughters, Barb and Pam.

The first photo is a framed announcement from the Lakeview Hotel.

Second is a Hallesy family portrait. Thomas Patrick and
Laura are at either end of the first row. Gordon (Dutchie)
is standing on the right behind his mother; Francis
(Frenchy) is at the other end behind his father.

*Third is Frenchy and Dorothy in their youth. Barb
says it reminds her of Bonnie and Clyde.*

CHAPTER 21

Prohibition In The EUP, Its Stills And Moonshine

The author Russell M. Magnaghi did some extensive research into the raucous history of Yooper Prohibition, with his book, 'Prohibition in the Upper Peninsula.' It's a great read and has an interesting history.

The Prohibition era was the period from 1920 to 1933 when the US prohibited the production, importation, transportation, and sale of alcoholic beverages. The alcohol industry was curtailed by a succession of state legislatures, and finally ended nationwide with the ratification of the 18th Amendment to the U.S. Constitution. It was ratified on January 16, 1919. Prohibition ended with the ratification of the 21st Amendment, repealing the Eighteenth Amendment on December 5, 1933.

Now at the time, we were led to believe that Prohibition would protect individuals and families from the "scourge of drunkenness." However, it had unintended consequences, including a rise in organized crime associated with the illegal production and sale of alcohol, an increase in smuggling, and a decline in tax revenue.

I always wondered what other people may have heard, and what other people may have read, and still what other people were told by our older generation, about "What was life really like during the Prohibition? And What were people really thinking about voting for something like that 18th Amendment into our daily life?" And what was life like in the EUP under Prohibition?

A still captured in Schoolcraft County

Even The Moonshiners of that period, and its many drivers who were employed seemed to be an exciting bunch of risk-takers, while violating the law, they were a likable bunch. I know my Dad enjoyed hearing their stories as a young boy. At least that's the way folklore presented them. There is no doubt, as you look at it today, it was definitely a battle among rural vs. urban life and a clash of cultures that was confronting American society at that time.

Many individuals within the prohibition movement associated the crime and morally corrupt behavior of American cities with their large, immigrant populations. Saloons frequented by immigrants in these cities were often frequented by politicians who wanted to obtain the immigrants' votes in exchange for favors such as job offers, legal assistance, and food baskets. Thus, saloons were seen as a breeding ground for corruption. So that was how it was in Detroit, and Chicago, but that's not the EUP, and that's where it created many challenges for local law enforcement, and the Coast Guard, Treasury Agents and the Justice Department.

The real crazy thing was, economist's from Yale and other major universities during the early 20th century were in favor of the enactment of the Eighteenth Amendment. They even predicted that prohibition would eventually happen in the United States for competitive and evolutionary reasons. In a backlash to the emerging reality of a changing American demographic, many prohibitionists subscribed to the doctrine of Nativism, in which they endorsed the notion that the success of America was a result of its white Anglo-Saxon ancestry. This belief fostered distrust of immigrant communities that fostered saloons and incorporated drinking in their popular culture. And that certainly was the picture in the EUP.

***Policemen inspect the equipment used in a clandestine
brewery during the Prohibition era.***

Yes, here in the EUP we had our stills, and we were known to make
some great moonshine. In the Gogomain Swamp in Keldon, and Lake Brevort
we had our drivers, and we had our still owners having their difficulties with
the Treasury Department and our local sheriffs. A few of them served their
2–3 years in the State prison. But the stills moved again, and they kept on
going, making their moonshine. As everyone knew, the law was going to have
their work cut out for them in the Upper Peninsula, and they did also here
in the EUP. It was a wild and wooly place where moonshiners, bootleggers,
and rumrunners thrived.

On a larger scale, Al Capone and the Purple Gang came north to keep Canadian whiskey passing through Sault Ste. Marie to Chicago and Detroit. Federal enforcement agent John Fillion double-crossed both his office and the bootleggers. The Grand Hotel on Mackinac Island survived due to gambling and fine Canadian whiskey brought in by rum runners, sometimes assisted by the Coast Guard. There was great corruption among the law enforcement profession. One story of corruption came out of Keldon. A local Keldon driver was caught, arrested and sentenced to two years in State Prison. The arresting officer was a deputy sheriff from Pickford and offered to help the man's wife, he would help reduce his sentence and arrange his release if she would have sex with him. She was quite aware of his corruption, and she set him up to repeat his offer with other police listening. He was then arrested but lost his job without any sentence or imprisonment.

In town, according to police records, there were several raids on people's homes, where wine and beer were being made, and yes, people were making their own alcohol. Stills did exist, supposedly in some older barns throughout the Soo. So, the winemakers and beermakers, along with those making their own white lightning, had to be extremely careful. No wonder, over time, this crazy law started to become a joke. As even those dry communities who willingly voted for Prohibition, and we had those in the EUP. Many of their residents had their own bars in the basement of their homes and drank freely. Public opinion was shifting. The Country was deciding to turn around, and to move back to what was more normal. Prohibition was simply wrong.

Here's a little ditty that Edward, the Prince of Wales, heard during his visit to Canada. He came across it in a border town:

"Four and twenty Yankees, feeling very dry,

Went across the border to get a drink of rye.

When the rye was opened, the Yanks began to sing,

" God bless America, but God save the King!"

Rum runners, bootleggers, and good old homemade winemakers kept many folks smiling a hundred years ago. No wonder the medical profession and the Catholic Church spoke out loudly against prohibition.

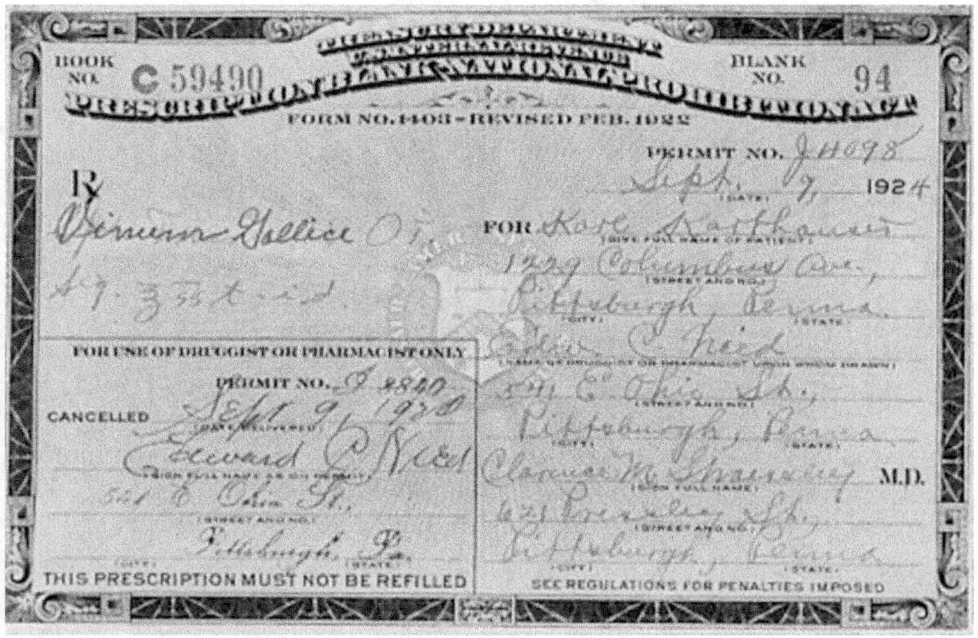

Prescription for medicinal alcohol during prohibition

CHAPTER 22

My Very Favorite Poems, With My Mother And Father

I've said several times, using Frank McCourt's definition for the love of his Irish Father. He said, "My Dad was my own Blessed Trinity." He also said, "He was God, the good Father, the good Son, and the Devil Himself." That was my dad too.

But he was as much a philosopher as he was a poet, and his favorite poem was written by William Butler Yeats. I remember the last time we recited it together. We were coming back to his house in Marquette from an AA meeting we attended. It was a very special time, God bless him.

THE HOST OF THE AIR

by WB Yeats

O'Driscoll drove with a song

The wild duck and the drake

From the tall and the tufted reeds

Of the drear Heart Lake.

And he saw how the reeds grew dark

At the coming of night-tide,

And dreamed of the long dim hair

Of Bridget his bride.

He heard it high up in the air,

A piper piping away,

And never was piping so sad,

And never was piping so gay.

And he saw young men and young girls

Who danced on a level place,

With Bridget his bride among them,

With a sad and a gay face.

The dancers gathered about him

And many a sweet thing said,

And an old man brought him red wine

And a young girl white bread.

But Bridget drew him by the sleeve

Away to the merry bands,

To old men playing at cards

With a twinkling of ancient hands.

He sat and played in his dream And thought not of evil chance, Until one bore Bridget his bride Away from the merry dance.

He bore her away in his arms,

The handsomest young man there,

And his lips and his neck and his arms

Were drowned in her long dim hair.

O'Driscoll scattered the cards

And out of his dream awoke:

And Old men and young men and young girls

Were gone like a drifting smoke;

But he heard high up in the air

I just loved reciting the poem, as did my father. It always brought tears to his eyes. I remember my brother Tim told me growing up he and Dad recited that poem together hundreds of times if they did it once. He recalled how Dad would whisper the part as he heard the pipers piping away.

I later read after I visited Ireland, up in Yeats Country in County Sligo, an explanation of what Yeats wrote. Here is the description of the Yeats School of Poetry.

"Picture yourself walking along the Irish countryside, and you see a celebration of men, women, and children. You take part in that celebration but at the blink of an eye, or like drifting smoke, they disappear (snap your fingers) just like that. You realize that these were not mortal people but fairies. And fairies have magical qualities.

Yeats wrote a poem about such things.

In the poem, the husband (O'Driscoll) finds mourners weeping for his wife when he comes home. Yeats mentions Hart Lake, which is located southwest of the town of Sligo.

Yeats tells a story about a man who works apparently as a kind of gamekeeper driving water-fowl from reed beds (perhaps for wild fowlers to shoot). He falls asleep and has a strange dream about his newlywed wife.

First, he sees a group of dancers, then he is invited to eat bread and drink wine, which has magical qualities. Next, he is invited to play cards with a band of old men, while his bride is stolen from him by a handsome young man. At this, he scatters the cards away and wakes, only to hear, still playing, the strange piping music he heard in his dream.

Seamus Heaney's 'When All The Others Were Away at Mass' is a poem that still has a special meaning in my life. As I mentioned in my previous books, my relationship with my mother was defined by how we communicated. She knew communicating with me directly would make no sense, so she figured she would use poetry, and I mean a lot of poetry. So, in my late teenage years until my mid 20s that became our Way. But as a youngster we had our special moments, and Heaney's poem strikes home as something that happened to me with my mother, a very special and private time.

When All The Others Were Away At Mass by Seamus Heaney has been named Ireland's best-loved poem from the past century. It was chosen from ballots cast by the public and announced by Irish President Michael D. Higgins. The third of eight sonnets in "Clearances," a series dedicated to the poet's mother, Margaret Kathleen McCann, the poem is featured in the recently published, Selected Poems (1966-1987), one of two new editions of Heaney's work that were arranged by the Nobel laureate himself.

When All The Others Were Away At Mass.

When all the others were away at Mass

I was all hers as we peeled potatoes.

They broke the silence, let fall one by one

Like solder weeping off the soldering iron:

Cold comforts set between us, things to share

Gleaming in a bucket of clean water.

And again let fall. Little pleasant splashes

From each other's work would bring us to our senses.

So while the parish priest at her bedside

Went hammer and tongs at the prayers for the dying

And some were responding and some crying

I remembered her head bent towards my head,

Her breath in mine, our fluent dipping knives –

Never closer the whole rest of our lives.

Seamus Heaney really knew how to write a personal poem. He chose a precious incident between mother and son that will always be remembered. As I read the poet's review of his work, both he and his mother were engaged in a domestic task, working in unison. Perhaps of more importance is that they had the time together to share in potato peeling while the rest of the family was away at Mass. 'I was all hers' are keywords as Seamus revealed at having a time of complete togetherness. And he had obviously seen solder melt and form droplets to fall away from the heated iron. And likewise, when the potatoes were peeled they would fall and the splash would break the silence of their intense communion and bring them to their senses. You can easily picture this intimate scene. I loved it, it happened to me.

CHAPTER 23

Civilian Conservation Corps

Preserving the Legacy of the Corps, 1933-1942.

One of the greatest enjoyments of my travels across the Upper Peninsula was chatting with the old folks about Logging in the UP, cutting the great White Pine, the stripping of the land, and the plantation of trees that followed with the creation of the CCC. It was often called Roosevelt's Tree Army by its critics, but some of the folks who worked there in the camps, as members making $30 per month, had a lot to say. The first thing is they had a job, then had a bed to sleep in, and to top it all off they had three square meals a day.

The Civilian Conservation Corps (CCC) was a voluntary government work relief program that ran from 1933 to 1942 in the United States for unemployed, unmarried men ages 18–25 and eventually expanded to ages 17–28. The CCC was a major part of President Franklin D. Roosevelt's New Deal that supplied manual labor jobs related to the conservation and development of natural resources in rural lands owned by federal, state, and local governments. The CCC was designed to supply jobs for young men and to relieve families who had difficulty finding jobs during the Great Depression in the United States. There was eventually a smaller counterpart program for unemployed women called the She-She-She Camps, which were championed by Eleanor Roosevelt

Poster by Albert M. Bender, produced by the Illinois WPA Art Project Chicago in 1935 for the CCC

CCC boys are leaving camp in Lassen National Forest for home.

Robert Fechner was the first director of this agency, succeeded by James McEntee following Fechner's death. The largest enrollment at any one time was 300,000. Through the course of its nine years in operation, 2.5 million young men took part in the CCC, which provided them with shelter, clothing, and food, together with a monthly wage of $30 (equivalent to $706 in 2023), $25 of which (equivalent to $588 in 2023) had to be sent home to their families

A CCC-built bridge across Rock Creek in Little Rock, Arkansas

The American public made the CCC the most popular of all the New Deal programs.

Sources written at the time claimed an individual's enrollment in the CCC led to improved physical condition, heightened morale, and increased employability. The CCC also led to greater public awareness and appreciation of the outdoors and the nation's natural resources, and the continued need for a carefully planned, comprehensive national program for the protection and development of natural resources.

In the state of Michigan, there were a total of 59 camps. Combined, they employed 11,800 young men in Michigan. Here in the EUP, we have two very large camps, one located in the Tahquamenon/Newberry area region of the state and another at RACO. The RACO camp, just west of Sault Ste Marie, was the very first CCC camp in the state, and Northern Michigan and the Upper Peninsula ended up having 41 of the 59 camps. Although most of the camps were located in National and State Forest's, a few were located in State Parks.

By 1942, when the CCC program ended, Michigan workers had planted 484 million trees, more than twice the amount of any other state. In the early 1960s, with initial reforestation largely completed, the Higgins Lake Nursery ceased operation.

CCC Camp Newberry

CCC Camp RACO

Pictures from the Tahquamenon Logging Museum

There have been doubts about the effectiveness of the CCC, but just look at our forests today and one should say thank you. Let's not forget during our great lumber boom our land was stripped bare, and over 3 billion seedlings were planted by the CCC. It is apparent to me that the CCC had a lasting effect on its enrollees. Life in the camps brought tangible benefits to the health, educational level, and employment expectancies of almost three million young Americans, and it also gave immediate financial aid to their families. Equally important were the intangibles of Corps life. The CCC gave its enrollees both a new understanding of their country and a faith in its future. Youths from the teeming cities learned something of rural America,

boys from farms and country hamlets became acquainted with the complex-
ities and ethnic variation of their land and its people. Both emerged from the
camp experience with a greater understanding of America, and of Americans.

Despite its shortcomings, the CCC was of the profoundest importance. It
was important because of its effect on the nation's national resources and the
health of its enrollees, and it is important to the story of reform in the United
States. It marked the first attempt by the federal government to provide some
specific solution for the problems of youth in an increasingly urban society.
In its makeshift, loose way it was a pathfinder, the precursor of more sophisticated programs and ideas. After the CCC came Roosevelt's National Youth
Administration, the attempts at providing federal aid to education pursued by
every post war president, and the complex of youth agencies which form such
an integral part of President Lyndon B. Johnson's war on poverty. Indeed,
the parallels between one of these, the Job Corps, and the CCC are striking.
To be sure, Job Corps is a far more sophisticated agency than the old CCC,
its functions are at once more specialized and more diverse. Nevertheless,
its enrollees, too, are unemployed young men between the ages of eighteen
and twenty-five years; they, too, live in camps, sometimes old CCC sites
first used over thirty years ago; they, too, work in the woods. Through its
successes as well as its shortcomings, the CCC has surely provided, in this
instance, a concrete example for others to follow.

Though the CCC is dead, it has not been forgotten. As Arthur M.
Schlesinger, Jr., wrote, it has " left its monuments in the preservation and
purification of the land, the water, the forests, and the young men of America."

Stripped land requiring reforestation, Once a

full forest before complete decimation.

And to add a little levity to the title. There were several songs written and sung about the CCC, some of course patriotic and building character, but there was always the protest song. A little sarcastic humor is always good for the soul. Here is a song called Loveless C.C.C.

Loveless C.C.C.

Copied from the text in Herman Beeman's ballet book. Song written by Beeman's bunkmate in Brokenair CCC Camp, Oklahoma, 1937.)

Why did I ever Join the C.C.C.?

Oh, why did I join the C.C.C.

Why did I join the C.C.C.?

This old hard labor's killing me.

They treat me like a dirty dog

I have to slave down in a log

And they feed me like a hog

Oh, why did I join the C.C.C.?

I haft to work most ever day

Five bucks a mounth is my pay

I'm just a wasting my life away

Oh, why did I join the C.C.C.?

The Lieut. sure is hard-boiled

His hands and clothes are never soiled

When I come in all day I've toiled

Oh, why did I join the C.C.C.?

These O. D. clothes sure is hot

They'll make you scratch a whole lot

They'll make you wish you'd never got

Into this old C.C.C.

Note: the same boy wrote another parody, this time to the familiar cowboy song, of which Beeman remembered only the following verses (which he thinks were all that were composed but isn't sure).

There's an empty cot in the barrack tonight

There's a C.C.'s head hanging low.

The ax and saw hang on the wall.

Now he's gone where the C.C. boys go.

There's a place for every C.C.

But the facts, as they say, remain the facts—it is a fact that our country's decimated forests were prioritized, with over 3 billion trees planted nationwide and 500 million in Michigan.

- It is a fact that over 125,000 miles of roads and trails were built in over 800 parks nationwide.

- It is a fact that the CCC constructed over 6 million erosion control structures, to prevent soil erosion.

- It is a fact that 13,000 miles of hiking trails that were built transformed our national parks, national forests, and state parks. And many state park systems have advanced significantly.

- It is a fact that the CCC provided work, meals, shelter, uniforms, and a monthly wage for 2.5 million of our Country's unemployed, unmarried young men from 1933-1942.

- It is a fact that the CCC spent 6 million workdays fighting Forest fires.

Call it Roosevelt's Tree Army if you wish, call it a Nation Relief program if you wish, but the bottom line cannot be denied, in total, there were 194 CCC work camps in 94 national parks and 697 camps in 881 state and local parks across the US. And that's called IMPACT.

CHAPTER 24

The National Anthems Of The Countries I Love—
The United States And Canada

It is only fitting that as a Finale to finish this book, I print both of the Country anthems to me that matter. I love these Countries and what they have both given me in my lifetime. As I have said earlier, I have flown 2.7 million air miles, I have worked in 37 of our States, and became quite acquainted with five major cities, and Provinces in Canada working there, and living there, raising funds for their economies. My only wish is I could still acquire dual citizenship in Ireland, as that country too has a strong family appeal. A tribute to my family, who for years loved the meaning of America, but felt in exile from Ireland.

But as a salute to the very fine people both of the US and Canada which I hold dual citizenship in each Country. My love, regard, thanks, and respect.

US National Anthem Lyrics

Francis Scott Key, 1814

O! say can you see by the dawn's early light,

What so proudly we hailed at the twilight's last gleaming,

Whose broad stripes and bright stars through the perilous fight,

O'er the ramparts we watch'd, were so gallantly streaming?

And the rockets' red glare, the bombs bursting in air,

Gave proof through the night that our flag was still there;

O! say does that star-spangled Banner yet wave,

O'er the Land of the free and the home of the brave?

Canadian National Anthem

Calixa Lavallée, a Quebecois concert pianist, composed the melody in 1880. The Lyrics to 'O Canada'

English version:

O Canada!

Our home and native land!

True patriot love in all of us command.

With glowing hearts we see thee rise,

The True North strong and free!

From far and wide,

O Canada, we stand on guard for thee.

God keep our land glorious and free!

O Canada, we stand on guard for thee.

O Canada, we stand on guard for thee.

French version:

Ô Canada!

Terre de nos aïeux,

Ton front est ceint de fleurons glorieux!

Car ton bras sait porter l'épée,

Il sait porter la croix!

Ton histoire est une épopée

Des plus brillants exploits.

Et ta valeur, de foi trempée,

Protégera nos foyers et nos droits.

Protégera nos foyers et nos droits.

CHAPTER 25

A Final Salute

So dear readers, this ends my Trilogy, and I salute those of you who have read my books and gotten something from them. It's taken these four Books to help define major parts of my life, my own personal struggles, and my sheer enjoyment of collecting songs and stories of our past. When I first began ten years ago, writing part one of 'The Sounds and Smells of My Childhood', I wanted to leave behind for my children and grandchildren. I wanted them to know how life and society was back then, how people treated one another, how patriotism and love of Country mattered. Things were just simpler in so many ways even with our own difficulties, but there was a sense of decency and respect that appears to be lost today. Part II was a continuation with more of the nostalgia of the 1950s and filled with tons of local history. It was important for me to tell this story so that at least it has been recorded for posterity.

As I wrote in my next book, 'My Road to Sobriety,' a major part of my recovery and overcoming my addiction to alcohol, was to become a student of our philosophers and great poets and writers. I used their sayings and writings throughout my career to motivate the local leadership of towns, cities, regions, and states and then raise the funds that would implement how they wanted their locations to grow. Be it a new airport, a new intercity light rail system, a new convention center, or just new primary jobs.

George Bernard Shaw's spirit was with me always, as I was using his words. His greatest quote, I used a million times, it worked to keep me on my sobriety road. Equally important, it got folks and communities to move forward. "A life spent making mistakes, is not only more honorable but more useful than a life of doing nothing." My point here was, it is time to be bold, with no meanness, no fear, and no surrender. That it was ok to dream, and as Ziglar said, "If you can dream it, you can achieve it."

Or, as my favorite Emerson said, "Nothing great was ever achieved without enthusiasm." So be enthusiastic! He would finish with his knockout statement, "it's not so much where we stand today those matters, but in which direction we are heading, If our purpose in life is to sail to the Port of Heaven, then we must set our sails, sometimes with the wind, and sometimes against it, but not lay at bay at anchor."

My final book, 'Songs and Stories from A Canadian Yooper', was simply fun. It was sheer enjoyment, and although I wrote it for the fun of it, it too was quite historical. To me, all the stories had great meaning, and I met some great people along the way as I wrote it. I enjoyed the three guest writers and reading their stories and experiences. They added so much value, humor, and history to the book. I again want to thank Shirley Patrick for her guidance and assistance.

But more than anything I wanted to directly counter our Yooper origins with our Western Yooper cousins, as our base is Canadian not Scandinavian.

To let people know we were Canadian, and part of Upper Canada for many, many years before the United States and England decided our fate with its

Boundary Commission. We are, proudly, Canadian Yoopers.

I enjoyed immensely the music and poetry I've used in each of my books. All of it is a real reflection of things that were given to me and really moved me. The people that sang those songs, and the people who recited those lovely poems have all been kept alive and remembered as my dad would say with my books. They were a major part of my Circle of Life. So here is my salute to those special people:

Let The People Sing

"Let the people sing their stories and their songs

And the music of their native land

Their lullabies and battle cries and songs of hope and joy

So join us hand in hand

All across this ancient land

Throughout the test of time

It was music that kept their spirits free Those songs of yours and of mine."

THANK YOU

ACKNOWLEDGMENT

I want to thank those who have been involved with assembling the various stories and songs I've used in the book. My sister Mary McCarthy, and Sister-in-law Jean McCarthy, my lifelong friend Fred Benoit, my nephew Brian Balmes and my brother Tim McCarthy. Significant assistance came from the Chippewa County Historical Society. This 104-year-old organization and its entire board are a treasure and resource of pictures and historical knowledge for the community. They were critical to my research. To my boyhood friend, BYREE, my good friend Donald Paul Byron for his tenacity in researching the infamous football game with St. Ignace and Loretto. You were right, Paul. Loretto won that game 33-13, thanks for telling me your story. RIP dear friend. Peter Campbell did some wonderful research that was terrific to make our Case to the State of Michigan. Peter has developed to be quite the author and historian himself. His historic work of developing the story of the Sault's hockey history, from 1900 to 2024, will be a treasure for all hockey lovers and all the citizenry of Sault Sainte Marie.

Go get it, Pete! Tony Bosbous, the former Mayor of the Sault, gave great input into a few stories, and his feedback into several chapters is appreciated. Tony Andary's hunting story is a delight. It's funny, historical, and very entertaining. It's a great remembrance of a young boy waiting his turn at "opening day". I hope you will enjoy it too. Tony and his lovely wife Nancy have been friends for a number of years, and he, like his father, is a genuine storyteller.

So, thanks everyone, I couldn't have done this without you. Not to be forgotten as they played a major role in my research were: Siri, Google, Wikipedia, Reddit, and several other internet connections.

But, it's the people who enjoy reading about our history. Without them, this task would have been impossible. Throughout my travels around the UP, I spoke with so many great people and story tellers, young and old. Special thanks to the Public libraries in towns throughout the UP. Thanks also to The Tahquamenon Historical Society and its Logging Museum for the historical research, pictures, and information they provided with great data on our logging history in the EUP. The Michigan Department of Transportation proved to be a great resource with its ferries and bridges. And thanks to the several authors who have written about life in the UP, its stories and folklore, its ghost towns. Most especially thank you to the author Russell M. Magnaghi for some of his extensive research into the raucous history of Yooper Prohibition.

And a special, special Thanks to Barbara Hallesy Wirt, and my family members, John, and his son, Ethan McDonald.

Barbara has been a lifelong friend, and she has agreed to write a chapter of her family business—Hallesy's Bar, in my book. Her retirement plans have always been to write a total family history, but it has been spawned by her willingness to write this first chapter. But, to go through that lovely traumatic recall of life is a big undertaking. I am so honored that she chose this outlet to begin the writing of her family history in business. It will go down as one of the finest books ever written about our town, and one of the great families in it.

And to my family, John and his son, Ethan McDonald. Thanks so much, guys. The McDonald Family has for all my life been so much a part of me. And to have father and son write about their fishing knowledge of truly one of the greatest places in the world to fish—our own St. Mary's River is a coup for those who want to try their luck. These boys know every bend and eddy in the river, every fly hatch, and every place where to wet a line. I know the reader will enjoy it. I certainly did.

And thank you for reading my books. I hope my stories and songs sparked some of your own great memories and thoughts. I'm still a Canadian Yooper., thanks be to God.

The author, Mike McCarthy